Seizing Moments
and Being Useful

Seizing Moments and Being Useful

The Development of a Single-Session Therapist

Windy Dryden

Rationality Publications

Rationality Publications
136 Montagu Mansions, London W1U 6LQ

www.rationalitypublications.com
info@rationalitypublications.com

This edition published by Rationality Publications
Copyright (c) 2025 Windy Dryden

The right of Windy Dryden to be identified as the author of this work
has been asserted in accordance with sections 77 and 78 of the
Copyright Designs and Patents Act 1988.

A catalogue record of this book is
available from the British Library.

First edition 2025

ISBN: 978-1-914938-40-5

Contents

Preface

My Development as a Single-Session Therapist

In this Preface, I will chart my developing interest in single-session therapy and describe how the material presented in this book documents my development in this regard. Before I do this, let me give a brief overview of my development as a counsellor/psychotherapist to provide a context.

What Drew Me to Become a Therapist

In school, I had a bad stammer and was teased by my fellow schoolboys for this. I became aware of my feelings of hurt and shame and thus learned about the inner world of emotional pain. I also became interested in why a boy with whom I was having a friendly private chat would, minutes later, join with other boys to taunt me for my speech impediment. This question led me to the decision to study psychology at university.

From Psychology to Therapy

At university, I volunteered to be a helper at Nightline, a telephone hotline for students in emotional distress. I enjoyed this and later volunteered for the Samaritans, a telephone hotline for members of the public in the UK who were suicidal. I enjoyed and resonated with this work and applied to train as a student counsellor in the last year of my PhD. After my initial counsellor training at the University of Aston in Birmingham, I became interested in what is now known as Rational Emotive Behaviour Therapy and trained in this approach in New York in the late 1970s.

What drew me to REBT was its attitudinal approach to understanding psychological problems and their resolution and

7

its 'let's get down to business straightaway' approach to helping people. Little did I realise it at the time, but the latter would be a prime reason why I became interested in single-session therapy about thirty-five years later.

Also, in the late 1970s, I undertook a Master's course in Psychotherapy at the University of Warwick. This broad, eclectic course gave me an overview of the field, which has stood me in good stead throughout my career.

Variety Is the Spice of Working Life

I have only had two full-time jobs in my working life (1975–2014). From 1975 to 1983, I was a Lecturer in Counselling at the University of Aston in Birmingham, where I trained people who wished to become student counsellors in further and higher education. I took voluntary redundancy from this position in 1983 and was appointed to a Senior Lectureship in Psychology at Goldsmiths University of London in 1985, becoming Britain's first Professor of Counselling in 1992. I retired from Goldsmiths in 2014.

The advantage of holding these positions was that it allowed me to do a variety of different things related to psychotherapy. Intrinsic to these two positions was that I had to lecture, train and supervise trainees on the programmes, as well as write and research. I have always maintained that it was essential for those who trained therapists to see clients themselves, and I have always adhered to this position. Thus, I have seen clients in individual, couples, and group therapy. I have worked in various settings – private practice, three private psychiatric hospitals, an NHS clinical psychology clinic, Relate and, latterly, an online health service offering 30-minute video-based counselling sessions (see Chapter 12). The fact that I have been involved in various psychotherapy roles has helped me remain fresh throughout my professional career.

On Becoming a Single-Session Therapist

In this section, I will consider some factors that influenced me to practise single-session therapy.

Live Demonstrations of Therapy

For many years, whenever I have offered training workshops, initially in-person and latterly online, I have always made it a point to do live demonstrations of therapy, whether Rational Emotive Behaviour Therapy (REBT) or, more recently, single-session therapy (SST). To date, I have done over 800 live therapy demonstrations (see Dryden, 2021a). These demonstrations taught me many things about what can be achieved in a single therapy encounter and laid the foundations for my later interest in SST.

Looking for a Challenge: On Retiring from Goldsmiths, University of London

In 2014, I retired from my full-time post as Professor of Psychotherapeutic Studies at Goldsmiths, University of London. I viewed this as a challenge and wanted to commit myself to an area of psychotherapy where I could make a difference. The choice was between single-session therapy or helping people with issues of procrastination.

Option 1: Promoting SST. In the early 2000s, I read Moshe Talmon's (1990) seminal book on single-session therapy. While I found it interesting, I did not resonate with Talmon's ideas and did not pursue them. In 2012, when I began to think about what I wanted to do post-retirement, I re-read Talmon's book, and this time, I was strongly drawn to his ideas. Obviously, the book had not changed, but I had. I was concerned about what I read about increasing waiting times for therapy and corresponding growing waiting lists for therapeutic help in NHS clinics in the UK.

From what I was beginning to learn about SST, I could see that introducing SST into NHS therapy agencies could help the many people who wanted brief therapeutic assistance. I was struck by the fact that whenever SST was introduced into therapy agencies, waiting times for help were reduced and waiting lists came down. In addition, I discovered first-hand from all the live therapy demonstrations that I had done that I could make a real difference to many people in a very short time without knowing anything about them and without subjecting them to needless pre-therapy assessment procedures. And if I could be useful to people in a single session, other therapists could do too.

Option 2: Establishing a clinic for people with procrastination issues. The second option I considered was setting up and running a clinic for people with procrastination issues. I had a long-standing interest in helping people with such issues (Dryden, 2000, 2022a) and was a good role model as I tend not to procrastinate in my own life.

When I discussed this situation with a trusted friend, he made the excellent point that if I set up a procrastination clinic, I would spend much time chasing people to get paid.[1] This helped tip the balance, and I committed myself to promoting SST after retiring from Goldsmiths.

Practising SST in Private Practice

In 2014, there were no training programmes in SST,[2] so I decided to draw upon my strengths[3] as a therapist when I began to practise SST. As I reflect on them, these strengths are:

- Being able to get to the heart of a client's nominated issue quickly;
- Promptly creating a therapeutic focus with a client and maintaining that focus throughout the session;
- Being able to form a good enough working alliance with a client in the session;
- Listening to what the client wants from the session and being led by the client's goals.

I have always had a small, part-time private practice and decided at that time to open my practice to potential clients who might be

---

[1] Subsequently, it occurred to me that I could ask people to pay in advance for therapeutic services. Later, I found a way to combine both interests (Dryden, 2024b).

[2] Subsequently, I took online training courses in SST at the Bouverie Centre, Melbourne in Australia and at the Association for Psychological Therapies in the UK.

[3] A typical SST strategy!

interested in single-session therapy. Influenced by Talmon (1990), I decided to offer clients a telephone conversation designed to help them prepare for the face-to-face session, which generally took place a few days after the telephone call.

This was pre-COVID-19, where very little therapy took place online. In doing it this way, I found that approximately 20% of clients found the pre-session telephone preparation conversation sufficient and did not need the face-to-face session. Then, during the COVID-19 pandemic, all therapy went online, and I replaced my pre-session telephone call with a pre-session form, the purpose of which was again to help clients prepare for the online session.[4]

After the pandemic, in general, much therapy is offered online and indeed for SST, most of my private clients want to be seen online as they hail from across the UK and Europe. Thus, my current practice of SST is as it was during the pandemic, where clients are asked to prepare for the session by form, and the session occurs soon after online.

The only difference I have found in this 'form-online' delivery system is that no clients have said completing the form was sufficient. Thus, they all proceeded to attending the online session.

Training and Supervising Others in SST

As I explained above, I have always had a variety of roles in psychotherapy, including training and supervising therapists. Given the fact that nobody was offering training or supervision in SST in the UK, I resolved to do so, and for the last ten years, I have run hour-long, two-hour long, half-day, full-day, two-day and certificate-level courses in SST. These have been mainly online, but recently, there has been an increase in agencies wanting in-person training. I have been engaged to offer training by several online therapy training organisations, such as Onlinevents, by university counselling services and by various

---

[4] Pre-COVID-19, I considered it important for the medium in which the preparation took place (by telephone) to be different from the session itself (in-person). During COVID-19, I retained this difference in medium. Thus, preparation took place in written/typed form and the session occurred online.

therapy agencies. Sometimes, when such services or agencies introduce SST into their therapy offerings to clients, they will ask me to supervise their counsellors, usually monthly. Such contracts tend to last for one or two years.

The NHS Pilot

As I explain in Chapter 1, if a person seeks therapy from the National Health Service in the UK, they will go to a service known as 'NHS Talking Therapies for Anxiety and Depression' and be assessed by a service representative who will determine what type of therapy they are suited for. Once this has been done, the person will have to wait to be offered an appointment, often for months. SST would not thrive in such a system.

I discovered this while participating in an SST trial that took place in the NHS.[5] Here, clients were only offered SST when their risk was deemed low, they wanted help quickly, and they had a specific problem or issue that the service considered they would benefit from focusing on. As such, only clients with 'simple' or 'minor' issues were offered SST. This contrasts with the experiences of therapists working in open-access, enter-now SST services where anyone who attends is offered a single session and clients with both 'simple' and 'complex' issues are helped. In the NHS, clients can't choose SST; they can only be referred to it. After the trial, the service continues to offer SST, but only 8–9% of their total clientele have it, and their therapists who volunteered for the pilot see about two clients a month. I believe this agency is not getting as much benefit from SST as it could. For this to happen,

- Clients need to select SST rather than be selected for it.
- All therapists should be expected to offer it, be trained to do so and have ongoing supervision in SST.
- SST should be integrated into the agency and given equal status (as seen by therapists and clients) with the other modes of therapy offered to clients. This won't happen if therapists are only seeing two clients a month.

---

[5] I trained those therapists who volunteered for the pilot in SST and supervised them for about a year.

While I had hoped that 'NHS Talking Therapies for Anxiety and Depression' services would offer people the opportunity to have SST by selecting it for themselves, this won't happen as long as the current suitability assessment procedures that are embedded in such services continue to hold sway.

Working for an Online Counselling Service

In Chapter 12, I discuss my experiences working as a counsellor for an online health service that offers clients 30-minute video sessions where the modal number of my sessions with 463 clients in March 2022–April 2023 was '1'.[6] Thus, I was able to bring a single-session mindset to this work and saw a great variety of people from across the UK, which has deepened my experience of and expertise in SST.

Writing

Since 1984, I have contributed to the psychotherapy and self-help literature by writing books, chapters and articles, and this has been the case over the last ten years that I have been involved with SST. My SST publications can be found in Appendix 1.

This Book

I wanted this book to give readers a sense of my development as an SST therapist, so most chapters appear in the order in which they were published. The exception is **Chapter 1**, which was published in 2019 and updated here. I thought that it was important for this book to begin with a general introduction to SST, without which readers may find it difficult to understand the remaining chapters.

Chapters 2 and 3 feature transcripts of my pre-SST single-session demonstration work using the principles and practices of Rational Emotive Behaviour Therapy (REBT).[7] In my commentaries on these sessions, I have shown what I would have done differently if I had approached the sessions while holding a

---

[6] See Figure 12.1 in Chapter 12.
[7] The session that I did in Chapter 2 originally took place in 1994 and that which appears in Chapter 3 took place in 2008.

single-session therapy mindset. The session that appears in Chapter 3 was with a young man seeking help for a procrastination issue and took place in 2008. The session that appears in **Chapter 4** was with a woman seeking help for a procrastination issue and took place in 2024. I have included the latter so the reader can directly compare the session where I did not bring the single-session therapy mindset to the session (Chapter 3) with the session where I did (Chapter 4).

The material in **Chapter 5** was initially published in four separate articles and focuses on the skills needed to conduct a single session from beginning to end. I have always taken a skills-based approach to therapy and welcomed the opportunity to bring this approach to SST to an audience perhaps unfamiliar with this mode of therapy delivery. I decided to collate this material, which appears in this book as a single chapter.

Chapter 6 features the in-person, demonstration single-session work I did at the UK CBT meetup group between 2012 and 2020 before COVID-19. This and my other demonstration work (see Dryden, 2021a) helped me hone my SST skills and prepared me for the work I later did for an online counselling service where sessions were 30 minutes long (see Chapter 12).

Chapter 7 features a focused discussion on what I call REBT-informed SST. I have included this chapter because when I do use approach-specific ideas and practices, they are often from REBT. Interested readers should contrast the approach outlined in this chapter with the work presented and discussed in Chapters 2 and 3, which I might describe as 'single-session REBT uniformed by SST'.

Chapter 8 briefly discusses the different terms that single-session work has gone by. I explain in this chapter why I favour the term 'ONEplus therapy', even though the more common term is 'single-session therapy'.

Chapters 9 and 10 discuss two significant concerns that therapists have in general about single-session therapy. In **Chapter 9**, I address a major fear that therapists who bring a more conventional therapy mindset to learning about SST have concerning this work. I call this the fear of 'opening up a can of worms'. It is so prevalent that I addressed it in a separate publication. In **Chapter 10**, I address another primary concern that this group of therapists have about SST: how to deal with client risk and minimise harm in this mode of therapy delivery. I wrote this piece especially for this collection of my writings.

As I have developed as a single-session therapist, trainer and supervisor, it has become increasingly clear to me that the mindset practitioners bring to the work is central to the effective practice of SST. Indeed, when therapists criticise SST, they usually do so from the perspective of a conventional therapy mindset. Thus, in **Chapter 11,** I present 28 features of the single-session therapy mindset as I see them.

Finally, in **Chapter 12**, I discuss the work that I did from March 2022 to April 2023 for an online counselling service. In doing so, I show how I used some of the features of the single-session therapy mindset discussed in Chapter 11 to inform my work. While I enjoyed the work, I could not continue it due to organisational constraints. While SST has the power to transform mental health services, it will only do so in environments conducive to its development.

I hope you will seize the moment to read this book and find its contents of use to you and your clients. I would value your feedback. Please send it to me at windy@windydryden.com

1

Single-Session Therapy: An Introduction

Overview

In this chapter,[8] I provide an introduction to single-session therapy (SST) and show how it can help meet client needs where the demand for services outstrips supply. I begin by providing some relevant definitions before considering the foundations of SST. I then compare the features of help provided at the point of need and the features of help provided at the point of availability. It is clear from this comparison that SST is consistent with the former. I then consider whether SST is a mindset, a mode of service delivery or a discrete therapeutic approach. I argue that it is the first two and not the latter. I then discuss the goals of SST before considering the issue of indications and contraindications for SST. A comprehensive discussion follows of the do's and don'ts of good practice in SST before I provide an example of an effective single-session therapy structure. I end the chapter by considering and responding to common misconceptions of SST.

Two Pathways to Seeking Help

Imagine this scenario. Samantha Smith had been struggling with problems of anxiety for several months, and after prompting from her family, she decided to see her seek help from her local NHS Talking Therapies for Anxiety and Depression service. When

---

[8] This chapter first appeared as Dryden, W. (2019). *Single-Session Therapy (SST) and One-At-A-Time (OAAT): Help at the Point of Need.* Rationality Publications. It is published here in updated form with the publisher's kind permission. In its updated form, it serves as an introductory framework to the remaining chapters in this book.

Samantha contacted this service, she was told that someone from the service would contact her within a few weeks to conduct a telephone assessment with her. This assessment took place, and the assessor concluded that Samantha was suffering from mild to moderate generalised anxiety disorder (GAD) and referred her for low-intensity CBT, which would either take the form of guided self-help or occur in a psychoeducational group.

Samantha was told that there would be a six-week wait for such help. If Samantha's GAD was assessed to be in the severe range, then she would have been referred for high-intensity CBT which would occur in a 1-to-1 setting and for which there would be a four to five month wait. Samantha was reluctant to opt for guided self-help and did not want to join a group. She preferred to see a CBT therapist 1-to-1. She was told that a special case would have to be made for such help and that she would be contacted in one week. Subsequently, Samantha was told that her request for 1-to-1 CBT was granted and she was offered an appointment in eighteen weeks. The time it took for Samantha to have her first therapy session after first making contact with the NHS service was twenty-one weeks.

Contrast this with what would happen if Samantha went to an agency that offers an open-access, enter-now option. She would decide that she wanted to talk to a mental health professional, go into the open-access, enter-now service, complete a brief intake form, and then have a session, usually less than an hour after arrival.

This chapter is based on the second approach to service delivery rather than the first.

What Is Single-Session Therapy?

I see single-session therapy as an intentional endeavour where the client and therapist agree to work together to help the client take away from the session what they want, knowing that the client can request more help after they have had an opportunity to implement what they have learned from the session. The important aspects here are as follows:

- **Intention**

The intention here is to help the client in one session, if possible. It is not to bring down waiting lists or to reduce waiting times for appointments, although these happen once SST is introduced into a therapy agency. Weir, Wills, Young & Perlesz (2008: 12) echoed this when they said SST 'is not a "one-off" therapy but rather a structured first session which attempts to maximise the client's first therapeutic encounter, understanding that it may be the only appointment the client chooses to attend, while entertaining the possibility of ongoing work'.

- **SST Is Ethical**

SST is based on informed consent. The client understands the intention of SST, as described above, and understands that more help is available if required. No client should be forced to have SST if they do not consent to it. In addition, no therapist should be compelled to practise SST if they don't want to.

- **SST by Design, Not by Default**

The view of SST outlined here is known as 'SST by design' or 'planned SST' rather than 'SST by default' or 'unplanned SST'. As Hymmen, Stalker & Cait (2013: 61) have written: 'SST refers to a conscious approach to make the most of the first session knowing it may be the only session the client decides to attend— not to the situation where there is an expectation that the client will attend multiple sessions but chooses to attend just one.'

- **More Help Is Available**

When they hear the term 'single-session therapy', many people think it means a therapy that lasts for a single session. Indeed, this may be the case if the client only wants to attend one session. However, in all other cases, the client will understand that they may have more help if requested. In such cases, they can opt for whatever help an individual therapist or therapy agency offers.

However, there are other views of SST that do see SST as one session. For example, single-session interventions are broadly defined as 'specific, structured programs that intentionally involve just one visit or encounter with a clinic, provider, or program' (Schleider, Dobias, Sung & Mullarkey (2020).

- *More Help Is Offered but Not at the End of the Session*

Unless there is a good reason to do otherwise, in most cases, the client will be encouraged to reflect on what they have taken away from the session, digest this learning, put it into practice and see what happens before they make a decision about further help. Thus, in my view, SST includes this period after the session. Some agencies implement this by saying to clients that they will be contacted two to three weeks after the session to see how they are getting on and determine if they need more help or not.

The Foundations of SST

Every approach to therapy and service provision is founded on a set of assumptions and/or principles. In this section, I will outline several such foundations of single-session therapy (SST).

Jeff Young's 'Three Findings' Foundations

Jeff Young (2018), a major developer of SST in Australia, has noted that the term 'single-session therapy' (SST) is an inaccurate one, but one that should be retained because of its ability to shock and stimulate discussion among therapists. Thus, SST challenges generally held beliefs about therapy such as (i) 'more is better'; (ii) real change happens slowly and gradually and (iii) effective therapy is built upon the therapeutic relationship, which takes time to develop.

However, rather than define SST, Young (2018: 44) outlined three findings that serve as some of its principal foundations.

- *Finding #1.* The most common number of service contacts that clients attend is one, followed by two, followed by three … irrespective of diagnosis, complexity, or the severity of their problem (Talmon, 1990).

- *Finding #2.* The majority (often about 70–80%) of those people who attend one session, across a range of therapies, report that the single session was adequate given their current circumstance (Talmon, 1990; Bloom, 2001; Campbell, 2012).

- *Finding #3*. It seems impossible to predict accurately who will attend one session and who will attend more, a proposition that has significant clinical and organizational ramifications. If it cannot be predicted who will attend one session and who will attend more, it follows that both possibilities need to be embraced simultaneously by both the worker and by their service system. That is, the first session should logically be conducted 'as if 'it may also be the last'.

Other Foundations

In addition to the above three findings, the following also serve as foundations of SST.

A brief encounter can be therapeutic. In life, we meet numerous people and most of these we will not see again. Occasionally, such 'brief encounters' can have a therapeutic impact on us, which may even last a lifetime. My own therapeutic 'brief encounter' came from listening to a radio interview with Michael Bentine, a British comedian, when I was in my mid-teens. Like me, Bentine had a stammer and during that interview, he was asked how he coped with stammering. He replied that he learned to develop the attitude, 'If I stammer, I stammer. Too bad!' which helped him with his anxiety about speaking in public. I really resonated with this attitude, and I have been applying it for almost 50 years. So, a 30-second segment from a radio interview half a century ago had an ongoing positive effect on me. The fact that it is possible that a brief therapy encounter can have a positive impact on a client is an important foundation of SST.

Therapy length is expandable. Parkinson's law of psychotherapy states that therapy expands and contracts to fill the time allocated to it (Appelbaum, 1975). Taking this law, Talmon (1993: 135) observed that, 'When the therapist and client expect change to happen now, it often does.' This principle is an important foundation of SST.

Human beings have the capability to help themselves quickly under specific circumstances. If human beings could only change slowly, then single-session therapy would not have been developed, let alone would they have flourished. For such change to occur, then four conditions need to be met: (i) knowledge of what to do to bring about change; (ii) having a committed reason to change; (iii) taking appropriate action; and (iv) being prepared to accept the costs of taking this action and of the resulting change.

Much can be achieved in SST if certain conditions are present. These conditions are:

- The client is ready to change, and the therapist can capitalise on their readiness.

- The therapist and client share realistic expectations for client change. They should neither expect quantum change (i.e. sudden, dramatic, and enduring transformations that affect a broad range of personal emotion, cognition, and behaviour) nor no change. Realistic expectations for change in SST include becoming unstuck and taking a few steps forward, setting a goal and having a plan to achieve it (see section on the goals of SST below)

- The therapist and client embark intentionally on SST (as discussed above).

SST reflects what a lot of clients or service users want from therapy agencies. In addition to the finding that the modal number of sessions that clients have internationally is '1', feedback from service users indicates that what they want is in keeping with what SST has to offer. Here is an example from a group of service users from an NHS Trust in north-east England. This group said they want:

- Clarity on what is on offer;
- Therapists to be realistic and not overstate choice;
- Therapists not to offer long-term therapy which feels overwhelming but to offer short-term pieces of work

which are reviewed so that the person can 'get out' without causing offence if that is what they want;

- Less therapy, but available when they want it;
- Therapists to link all the bits of the system together rather than therapy being removed from other services.

The therapist structures the session effectively. The SST therapist tends to bring to the work certain ideas about the session that help both them and their client get the most from the session. Thus, the effective SST therapist tends to view the session as complete in itself and plans the session according to the time available. However, most importantly, they have in mind a structure for the session that is flexible enough to incorporate modifications as needed. Hoyt (2000, 2018) has outlined one such structure. He argued that a single session has five phases: (i) a pre-session phase where induction and seeding occur; (ii) an early phase where alliance-building occurs, any pre-treatment change is discussed and built upon, and goal-setting takes place; (iii) a middle phase where novelty is introduced and solutions for change are discussed, selected and rehearsed; (iv) a late phase where action planning is done, relapse prevention occurs, and leave-taking takes place; and (v) a follow-through phase where follow-up and evaluation take place and the client returns for more help if needed.

Help provided at the point of need vs at the point of availability. One of the objectives of this chapter is to make a case for providing help at the point of client need. At the outset, I outlined two types of help provision: help at the point of need and help at the point of availability. Table 1.1 (p. 23) details the differences between the two more clearly. It is quite apparent from this table that SST practitioners are best placed to provide help at the point of client need.

Table 1.1 Differences between help at the point of need and
help at the point of availability

Help at the Point of Need	Help at the Point of Availability
• It is better to respond to client need by providing some help straightaway rather than by waiting to provide the best possible help.	• It is better to have clients wait for the best possible help than provide them with some help when they need it.
• Providing immediate help is more important than carrying out an assessment.	• Carrying out an assessment is more important than offering immediate help.
• Therapy should start immediately. A case formulation should be carried out only if needed.	• Therapy should only be carried out on the basis of a formulation of the case.
• Therapy can be initiated in the absence of a case history.	• It is important to take a case history before therapy is initiated.
• People have the resources to make use of help provided at the point of need.	• People have the resources to make use of help provided on the basis of a case formulation.
• Sooner is better.	• More is better.
• The best way to see if a client will respond well to therapy is by offering them therapy and see how they respond.	• The best way to see if a client will respond well to therapy is to offer them the most appropriate therapy based on a full assessment of their problems and on a formulation of their 'case'.
• Therapy can be initiated and risk managed if this becomes an issue.	• Risk must be properly managed before therapy is initiated.
• Appropriate therapy length is best determined by the client.	• Appropriate therapy length is best determined by the therapist.
• When a person does not return for another session this may well indicate that the person is satisfied with what they achieved, although it may be the case that they were dissatisfied with the help provided.	• When a person does not return for another session or before they have completed their 'course of treatment' they have dropped out of this treatment and it should be regarded as a bad outcome.

SST: Mindset and Mode of Service Delivery rather than a Therapeutic Approach

Most people in the SST field hold the view that SST is a mindset and/or a mode of service delivery and is definitely not a specific therapeutic approach. Thus, SST can be practised by therapists from a broad spectrum of therapeutic approaches (Hoyt & Talmon, 2014a; Hoyt, Bobele, Slive, Young, & Talmon, M, 2018; Dryden, 2024a).

The SST Mindset[9]

Jeff Young (2018) has outlined the features of this mindset or what he termed 'an SST-informed attitude to clinical work'. These features are:

- Approaching the first session 'as if' it could be the last; irrespective of diagnosis, complexity or severity.
- Exploring what each client wants to walk away with at the end of the session at hand (rather than the usual question of what the client wants from a course of therapy).
- Prioritizing what to focus on – negotiated between client and clinician, but largely client-led.
- Checking in at various points throughout the session to ensure the work is on track.
- Sharing directly, albeit in a tentative way, feedback, advice, strategies, commendations and information that the clinician feels is helpful, driven by the idea 'what would I want to share with this client if I never see them again?'.
- Providing resources and clarifying next steps.

The paradoxical nature of the SST mindset. Therapists need to understand that a key aspect of the SST mindset is its paradoxical nature. Thus, when clients know that more sessions are available, then they are more likely to be satisfied with one session knowing that they could return later if necessary.

---

[9] See Chapter 11 for an expanded discussion of the single-session therapy mindset.

Michael Hoyt, one of the field's leading figures has written eloquently on what happens when a 'one session only' approach to SST is taken. He said: 'Insistence produces resistance, imposition produces opposition, push produces pushback – so I think it is important to offer and invite, but not demand, one visit. In our studies of SST, we have been careful to refer to the "POSSIBILITY of one session being enough" and to say "When the first session MAY be the last"' (Hoyt, 2018: 157).

The pluralistic mindset in SST. Given that there is no specific approach to SST, this way of working can incorporate seemingly different approaches. It can do this because of its pluralistic nature or what may be referred to as working with 'both/and' rather than with 'either/or'. In discussing his own work, Talmon (2018: 153) wrote about working with opposite poles. For example:

- 'On one pole to validate a patient's story via empathic listening and on the other pole to challenge the problematic elements in the same storyline.
- On one pole, to increase a sense of hope or a realistic sense of optimism, and on the other pole helping him/her to accept certain parts of the harsh reality.
- There is an essential balance between offering neutral (and at times passive, silent) listening in one part of a session, and in another part, presenting active, focused questions.
- Similarly, between being non-directive at one point of the session, while at other times giving prescriptive-like directions.'

SST as a Mode of Service Delivery

As we have seen, some people in the field consider that SST is best viewed as a mode of service delivery and not an approach to delivering such services. As a service delivery mode, it utilises time in a very efficient way. Therapy is made available quickly, and the time spent in therapy is kept as short as possible according to what the client wants.

The Goals of SST

What can be realistically achieved by clients from SST? The following are examples of such goals (Dryden, 2024a).

- To get 'unstuck'.
- To take a few steps forward which may help them to travel the rest of the journey without professional assistance.
- To see that they have the wherewithal to achieve their goals.
- To select a possible solution to their problem.
- To gain an experience of the solution, if possible.
- To develop an action plan.

If clients have unrealistic goals regarding what they can usefully achieve from SST, their therapists should explain why this may be the case and attempt to set more realistic goals. If not, SST should not be initiated (Dryden, 2024a).

Who Is Suitable for SST?

Whenever I give a talk on SST, it is inevitable that I will be asked a question concerning for whom and for which problems it is indicated and not indicated. When I first became interested in SST and developed my own private practice-based approach I outlined a long list of indications and contra-indications for this way of working (Dryden, 2017). While on the one hand, this approach made sense, on the other hand, it raised the issue of carrying out a suitability-based assessment before therapy is initiated. As I showed earlier in this chapter in Table 1.1, one of the features of help provided at the point of need is that therapy begins at the very first moment of the therapy session. Given this, I modified my approach (Dryden, 2022a) and when a client contacts me, I outline the range of services that I offer, including SST and invite the client to choose SST if they think that this mode of therapy delivery is something they think they can utilise. If so, I initiate SST and suggest a different service if it becomes clear that the client would do better with this other service. This latter decision is a jointly taken one.

The main objection to using suitability-based criteria comes from SST as practised in 'open-access, enter-now' settings. A client who seeks help from such a clinic knows that they will be seen quickly and that this may be the only session that they have. They know that it is not the first session of a series of sessions stretching into the future. The therapist will see the client without knowing anything about them, the nature of their problem or what help they are seeking. The fact that the therapist is prepared to see the client under such conditions suggests that suitability-based assessment is not necessary and some would say not even desirable as it would provide a barrier between help sought and help offered.

Jeff Young (2018: 44) argued that the best response to the 'who is suitable?' question 'is to avoid having to answer it by embedding SST in the service system so that clients can return if they want to. Embedding SST into the service system so that all services the organization normally provides are available following an initial session, conducted as if it may be the last, allows the practitioner and the organization to avoid the "difficult if not impossible" decision of who is suitable and who is not suitable for a "one-off" session.' Additionally, as discussed above, attempting to determine who will attend once and who will attend further sessions is a difficult enterprise and one that shows that clinicians are not good at making such determinations.

SST Occurs in a Context

Before I discuss the practice of SST in detail, I want to make the point that this practice takes place in a context which needs to be understood. Talmon (2018: 150–1) notes that a 'one-at-a-time approach is embraced successfully where the need is much larger than the supply and where the therapists are working as a team with training and research being an active part of the process, and where the therapist's income is not based on a fee-for-time nor based on the assumption that more is always better'. However, when SST has been introduced into an agency by one or two enthusiasts who are not supported by most practitioners working in that environment and with administrative support at a minimum, then it will not flourish in the agency. Please bear this in mind while reading about the practice of SST. See Weir et al., (2008) for suggestions on how to implement SST into a service.

Good Practice in SST

A number of people in the SST field have put forward suggestions about what constitutes good practice in SST (e.g. Bloom, 1981, 1992; Talmon, 1990, 1993; Hoyt, Rosenbaum & Talmon, 1992; Slive & Bobele, 2011, 2014; Dryden, 2024a). Table 1.2 outlines many of these suggestions for good SST practice.

Table 1.2   Elements of good practice in SST

The effective SST therapist:

- *Engages the client as quickly as possible.*
- *Develops rapport through the work.*
- *Takes their time. The therapist and the client have sufficient time to achieve something useful in the session.*
- *Encourages the client to understand the nature of SST, what is possible and what is not and to choose whether or not they want SST.*
- *Is overt and collaborative with clients when deciding how much therapeutic contact is required.*
- *Is client-centred.* Clients are experts in reporting what kind of and how much change is important for them at any particular time. So, the therapist needs to focus on what the client wants.
- *Speaks clearly and at a rate which maximises the client's participation and understanding.*
- *Whenever practicable, explains what they are doing.* However, it is important that they are not obsessive about doing so.
- *Asks and explores what the client wants from the session rather than from therapy.* In doing so, they are fully aware that therapy may last for only one session.
- *Is active directive while encouraging the client's active participation in the process.*
- *Is focused and helps the client stay focused.*
- *Interrupts the client to preserve the session focus once negotiated when necessary.* The therapist should give a prior rationale for doing this and elicit the client's agreement. When interrupting the effective therapist does so with tact.

Table 1.2 continued

- *Keeps checking that they and the client are on the right track.* Thus, the therapist should shift the agenda to meet the client's concerns.
- *Adopts a solution-oriented stance, but when necessary, is problem-focused.* Many SST therapists practice solution-focused therapy where the focus is on 'solution talk' and not 'problem talk' (Furman & Ahola, 1992). However, as we have seen SST is practised by therapists from diverse orientations and in some a focus on problems is deemed helpful in SST. So, while it is difficult to think of SST that is not solution-oriented, the therapist should feel free also to focus on problems if this helps the selection of suitable solutions.

[The next two items are relevant for SST therapists who deal with client problems]

- *Elicits the problem from the client's perspective.*
- *Assesses the problem.*
- *Elicits the client's goal/preferred future and keeps focused on this.*
- *Ensures that this forward focus is underpinned by a value if possible.*
- *Asks what the client is prepared to sacrifice to achieve the goal/preferred future.*
- *Bridges to the future whenever possible.*
- *Encourages the client to be specific as possible but be mindful of opportunities for generalisation.*
- *Makes liberal use of questions.*
- *Ensures that the client answers the questions they are asked.*
- *Gives the client time to answer questions.* The therapist should remember that they have more time than they may think.
- *Checks out the client's understanding of and reaction to substantive points that they have made to the client.*
- *Identifies and responds to the client's doubts, reservations and objections including those that may be expressed non-verbally.*
- *Identifies and makes use of the client's strengths.*
- *Identifies the client's previous attempts to solve the problem.* The therapist should capitalise on the client's successful attempts and distance themself from the client's unsuccessful attempts.
- *Identifies and utilises the client's learning style, if possible.*
- *Identifies and make use of the external resources available to the client.* Factors external to therapy can be as important as those internal to therapy and sometimes more so.
- *Looks for ways of making an emotional impact.* However, they should not push to bring about an emotional response.
- *Encourages the client to take at least one meaningful point from the session and to have a plan to implement this point.*

Table 1.2 continued

- Helps the client to select a possible solution to their problem that makes most sense to them and fits their life situation.
- Encourages the client to practise the solution in the session if possible.
- Helps the client to plan to implement the solution in their everyday life and encourages them to determine how this goes before they seek additional help.
- Encourages the client to summarise the session and they should themself add any missing points.
- Ties up any loose ends.
- Agrees criteria for further sessions with the client.
- Plans for a follow-up with the client.

What to Avoid Doing in SST

There are a number of therapeutic practices that, while useful in certain situations, are generally to be avoided in SST. Other practices are generally not useful in therapy, but the time-sensitive nature of SST means that some therapists may be prone to use them. Practices to avoid in SST are outlined in Table 1.3 (see next page).

Getting SST off on the Right Foot

When SST is practised in open-access, enter-now clinics, then the therapist and client need to get down to work immediately. However, when SST is by appointment, the client has an opportunity to do some preparatory work to get the process off on the right foot before they meet with their therapist. I discuss one approach to this, which is an example of what Hoyt (2000, 2018) refers to as the pre-session phase of SST where induction and seeding occur.

An Example of a Pre-Session Form

Table 1.4 (p. 32) presents a form which I send to clients who have requested SST. This is designed to help them to prepare for the session so that they can get the most from it. I invite them to send me their completed form before our session so I can see their thinking.

Table 1.3   Practices to avoid in SST

- *The therapist should not*[10] *take an elaborate history.* If the therapist does so, this may take up the entire session and they won't have time to do any therapeutic work with the client.
- *The therapist should not let the client talk in an unfocused, general way.* While
- certain clients may gain benefit from a single session of unfocused exploration, most won't.
- *The therapist should not spend too much time in non-directive, listening mode.* The exception to this is when a client says that the best way the therapist can help them is just to listen.
- *The therapist should not develop rapport independent of the task of SST.* In SST,
- showing a client that the therapist is keen to help them as quickly as possible is perhaps the best way to strengthen the therapeutic bond.
- *The therapist should not assess where not relevant.* When the therapist assesses the client's problem assessment should stay focused on the problem.
- *The therapist should not carry out an elaborate case conceptualisation.* There is not sufficient time in SST for such a conceptualisation to be done. This poses a difficulty for some CBT therapists who hold that therapy needs to be conceptualisation-driven.
- *The therapist should not assume that the client knows what the therapist is doing or why they are doing it.* Explicitness and clarity are hallmarks of good SST.
- *The therapist should not rush the client.*
- *The therapist should not ask multiple questions.* This is a specific sign that the therapist is rushing.
- *The therapist should not leave the client hanging at the end of the session.* Session closure is important.

Of course, not all of the information provided by a client in the pre-session form is used in a single session. However, it is there for the therapist and client to use if needed.

An Example of the Structure of a Single Session

You may be wondering what the structure of a single session looks like. In what follows, I present an example of such a structure used by one counselling agency in the United Kingdom.

---

[10] In this table, I use the term 'should not' to mean 'ideally should not'.

Seizing Moments and Being Useful

Table 1.4 Pre-session form[11]

I invite you to fill in this form before your session with me. This will help you to prepare for the session so that you can get the most from it. It also helps me to help you as effectively as I can. Please return it by email attachment before our session. Be brief and concise in your answers.

1. **What is the issue that you want to focus on in the session?**
   Be concise. In one or two sentences get to the heart of the problem, if possible.

2. **Why is this significant?**
   What's at stake? How does this affect your life? What is the future impact if the issue is not resolved?

3. **What is your goal in discussing this issue in the session?**
   What are the specific results you would like to achieve by the end of the session that would give you the sense that you have begun to make progress on the issue?

4. **Why now?**
   Why are you seeking help for this issue at this time?

5. **How have you tried to deal with the issue up to this point?**
   What steps, successful or unsuccessful have you taken so far in addressing the issue?

6. **What are the strengths or inner resources that you have as a person that you could draw upon while tackling the issue?**
   If you struggle with answering this question, think of what people who really know you and who are on your side would say.

7. **Who are the people in your life who can support you as you tackle the issue?**
   Name them and say what help each can provide.

8. **What help do you hope I can best provide you in the session? Please check the main one. Do not check more than one box.**

   ☐ Help me to develop greater understanding of the issue

---

[11] On the actual form there are boxes after each item in which the person can write their responses.

☐ Help me by just listening while I talk about the issue
☐ Help me to express my feelings about the issue
☐ Help me to solve an emotional or behavioural problem; help me get unstuck
☐ Help me to make a decision
☐ Help me to resolve a dilemma
☐ Help me by signposting me to the most appropriate service for my situation
☐ Other (please specify):

Before attending, the client knows the service runs on SST lines. This means that while the therapist will try to help them deal with the problem in the session, further sessions are available.

- The therapist begins by explaining the service and the amount of time that the client has with them.
- The therapist explains the service's confidentiality policy and refers the client to its written policy statement if they require more detailed information.
- The therapist asks: 'What issue do you want to discuss with me today?'
- The therapist and client agree on the client's goal for the session.
- The therapist and client identify the help the client wants.
- The therapist and client agree on a focus based on the above three issues.
- The therapist assesses if the client is at risk (suicide/self-harm or harm to others) and takes appropriate action.
- The therapist asks, 'People usually try to resolve a problem themselves. What things have you tried?'
- The therapist encourages the client to continue to use strategies that they have found helpful and discourages the future use of unhelpful strategies.
- The therapist asks, 'What inner strengths and resiliency factors do you have that it would be useful for me to know about that might help you deal with the problem?' If necessary, the therapist educates the client about key strengths and resiliency factors (e.g., strong family relationships and friendships, positive outlook, spiritual

convictions, sense of hope, feelings of personal control, creativity, persistence and humour). The therapist explains the role of inner strengths and resiliency factors as crucial components of the process of moving forward.

- The therapist asks, 'What external resources can you make use of in dealing with your prioritised concern?' The therapist asks in particular about people who may support the client through the change process and relevant agencies who may provide help.

- The therapist then asks, 'What would be the smallest change needed to show you that things are heading in the right direction?'

- It is here that the therapist and client search for a solution which may include the therapist offering approach-based insights as well as what the client thinks will be helpful.

- Once a possible solution has been agreed upon the therapist encourages the client to practice the solution in the session.

- The therapist helps the client to develop an action plan, perhaps negotiating a specific task to initiate the change process.

- The therapist encourages the client to ask any questions which are answered before bringing the session to a close. In particular, the therapist might ask a question such as, 'What question(s) do you wish you had asked me when you got home today?'

- The therapist encourages the client to tell them anything about the *issue* that later they might regret not saying. In doing so, care should be taken that the client does not bring up a new issue.

- The therapist draws the client's attention to resources in the service's resource material or to 'apps' as appropriate.

- The therapist encourages the client to reflect on what they have learned, digest it, take appropriate action and let time pass. Then, if the client needs more help, they can seek it from the service.

- Finally, appropriate follow-up and evaluation are organised.

Misconceptions of SST

As noted earlier, Jeff Young (2018) views the term single-session therapy as something of a misnomer which should be retained because it serves as a catalyst for important debates about service delivery and what clients actually want from therapy as opposed to what clinicians they should have. However, SST is a term that therapists new to this field often have misconceptions about (Weir et al., 2008; Young, 2018). In this final section, I will detail some of these misconceptions and put the record straight[12].

SST is a Model of Therapy in Itself

As I argued earlier, SST is best seen as a mindset or an attitude towards clinical work or a mode of service delivery. It is not a discrete therapy model or therapeutic approach.

SST is the Answer to Everything

As Young (2018) has noted SST is a mode of service delivery that stands with other modes of service delivery. Thus, at the Bouverie Centre in Melbourne, Australia where Young was Director, all new clients have a single session and then decisions are made collaboratively about what further therapy the client needs if any. Here, SST is seen as an entry hub. It is definitely not seen as the answer to all clinical problems.

SST Is a Quick Fix

The Cambridge Dictionary Online defines a quick fix as 'something that seems to be a fast and easy solution but is, in fact, not very good or will not last very long'. As discussed in the section on the goals of SST, the purpose of this mode of service delivery is to help the person get unstuck or take a few steps forward towards their goal. In addition, it helps the person see that they have internal strengths and external resources that they can call upon to address their problem. The client is encouraged to try out an agreed solution to a problem and see what transpires and to make a further appointment if further help is needed. This is far from a 'quick fix'.

---

[12] See Dryden (2022c) for a comprehensive discussion of misconceptions held about SST.

SST Is Better than Other Modes of Service Because It Saves Money

There is no clear evidence that SST as a mode of service delivery is cheaper to run than other modes, such as time-limited or ongoing therapy, but even if there were, this is not a sound clinical rationale for its employment. As already mentioned, SST is best seen as a way of approaching clinical work that stands alongside and may feed into other delivery modes. It does not seek to compete with these other modes. Additionally, it is the intention of SST proponents to provide what clients most want rather than trying to save money. What does tend to happen when SST is introduced into an agency is that waiting times ae reduced for client appointments, which is appreciated by both clients and therapists.

SST Means a Restriction on Therapy Sessions

If a therapy agency has sufficient resources to offer all clients what they need, services would not need to be restricted. However, even under these circumstances, it is clear from the data that many clients will still choose to attend one, two or three sessions (Hoyt & Talmon, 2014b; Young, 2018). So, even when there is a reason to restrict the number of therapy sessions, most clients will still choose to attend very briefly. The main point here is that the provision of SST does not and should not mean that certain clients should not receive more help if they need it and want it. When clients receive such help, therapists should ideally continue to offer to be client-focused, whether that help is short-term or longer-term.

SST Means One Session

As I have already discussed, while there are some people in the SST community who define SST as one session and one session only (Schleider et. al., 2020), most people in the field recognise that SST does not preclude further sessions. For example, Cummings (1990) notes that single-session therapy is a good example of intermittent therapy through the life cycle, where a client may have a series of single sessions at various critical points in their life. In addition, so-called 'one-at-a-time (OAAT) therapy' that is practised in many UK universities may involve one session but does not preclude further sessions, albeit held one at a time.

SST Is 5, 10 or More Sessions 'Distilled' into One

This criticism of SST implies a speeded-up approach to therapy where the therapist crams a great deal of work into a single session. While a single session of therapy does have its own beginning, middle, and ending phases (Hoyt, 2018), this process takes full account of the integrity of the single session and does not seek to condense much longer therapy into one session. You can only do one session in one session.

SST Is the Same as Crisis Intervention

While SST is an appropriate mode of service delivery for clients in crisis, it is not equivalent to crisis intervention. It can and is used for clients who are not in crisis and can often help clients stave off such crises.

SST Is Simpler than Longer-Term Therapy Because It Is Brief and Focused

While this may be the case, the converse may also be true. Both modes of therapy require the therapist to have well-developed, albeit different therapeutic skills. Each therapy mode has its own complexity.

SST Is for Everyone

While anyone may turn up at an open-access, enter-now clinic, it does not mean that SST is for everyone. As already discussed, a single session may be given to all who seek help at such a clinic, and if a more appropriate service is indicated, then a jointly agreed referral is made. At the Bouverie Centre in Melbourne, Australia, everyone gets a single session, and further work, if needed, is provided by the same therapist, not referred out. Young (personal communication, 12/1/19) states that 'longer term work is part of the outcomes of an initial session conducted using the SST service delivery approach. For example, in our service, our initial research showed 50% of SST clients decided on attending only 1 session, 25% a further "single session" and 24% ongoing work, all of which was provided by the same therapist'.

SST Is Only Suitable for Clients Facing Simple Problems

Given that clients with a range of problems from the simple to the complex have sought help from and benefitted from SST this criticism comes more from therapists than from clients or service users. The latter have shown a high degree level of satisfaction with the services that they have received (Hoyt & Talmon, 2014b; Hoyt et al., 2018).

I hope that you have found this introduction to SST valuable. If you would like to deepen your understanding of the field, I have provided a set of recommended readings most of which are in publication date order, followed by a listing of other resources cited in the text.

Recommended Reading

Dryden, W. (2022). *Single-Session Integrated CBT (SSI-CBT): Distinctive Features. 2nd Edition.* Routledge.
An updated outline of the author's CBT-based SST model as practised in a private practice setting.

Dryden, W. (2024). *Single-Session Therapy: 100 Key Points and Techniques. 2nd Edition.* Routledge.
An updated overview of the field is provided as seen by the author.

Hoyt, M.F. (2025). *Single-Session Therapy: A Clinical Introduction to Principles and Practices. Routledge.*
Michael Hoyt, together with Robert Rosenbaum, joined Moshe Talmon at Kaiser Permanente in Northern California to pioneer the first study on planned SST. Since then, Hoyt has remained at the forefront of SST and brief therapy and this book provides a wealth of information for SST practitioners.

Slive, A., & Bobele, M. (eds). (2011). *When One Hour Is All You Have: Effective Therapy for Walk-in Clients.* Zeig, Tucker & Theisen.
This is an important text that focuses on the development and running of walk-in services and the nature of effective therapy in these settings. Please note that these services are now referred to as 'open-access, enter-now' services.

Talmon, M. (1990). *Single Session Therapy: Maximising the Effect of the First (and Often Only) Therapeutic Encounter.* Jossey-Bass.
This book initiated general interest in SST. It is a classic text and one that should be read first by those wanting to understand the field's roots.

Proceedings of the Four International Symposia on SST

Hoyt, M.F., & Talmon, M. (eds). (2014). *Capturing the Moment: Single Session Therapy and Walk-in Services.* Crown House Publishing Ltd.
Contains papers and addresses from the 1st international symposium on SST that took place in Melbourne, Australia in 2012 plus others addressing theoretical and technical SST issues.

Hoyt, M.F., Bobele, M., Slive, A., Young, J., & Talmon, M. (eds). (2018). *Single-Session Therapy by Walk-In or Appointment: Administrative, Clinical, and Supervisory Aspects of One-At-A-Time Services.* Routledge.
Contains papers and addresses from the 2nd international symposium on SST that took place in Banff in Canada in 2015.

Hoyt, M.F., Young, J & Rycroft, P. (eds). (2021). *Single Session Thinking and Practice in Global, Cultural and Familial Contexts: Expanding Applications.* Routledge.
Contains papers and addresses from the 3rd international symposium on SST that took place in Melbourne, Australia in 2019.

Cannistrà, F. & Hoyt, M.F. (eds). (2025). *Single Session Therapies: Why and How One-At-A-Time Mindsets Are Effective.* Routledge.
Contains papers and addresses from the 4th international symposium on SST that took place in Rome, Italy in 2023.

For those interested in implementing SST, the following sources are valuable.

Weir, S., Wills, M., Young, J., & Perlesz, A. (2008). *The Implementation of Single Session Work in Community Health.* The Bouverie Centre, La Trobe University.

Young, J., Rycroft, P., & Weir, S. (2014) Implementing SST: Practical Wisdoms from Down Under. In M.F. Hoyt & M. Talmon (eds), *Capturing the Moment: Single-Session Therapy and Walk-in Services* (pp. 121–40). Crown House Publishers.

Young, J., Weir, S., & Rycroft, P. (2012). Implementing single session therapy, *Australian and New Zealand Journal of Family Therapy,* 34(2), 69–74.

2

A Single REBT Session with a Woman Who Also Had a Single REBT Session with Albert Ellis (1994)

Preamble

In the summer of 1994 in New York, a woman I shall call 'Susan' asked for a therapy session with Albert Ellis to address her love life. Susan was married with two teenage children. She was reared in a strict Christian sect, married a man from the same tradition, and they reared their children in that tradition. However, Susan had become lovers with an REBT[13] therapist I shall call 'Stan' who was attending an REBT practicum in New York that summer. As Susan's husband was not willing to continue the current arrangement where she could stay married and have her relationship with Stan at the same time, she was in a quandary about whom to leave, her husband or her lover. Shortly after her session with Ellis, Stan asked me to see Susan for a single session as I was in New York as a member of the Albert Ellis Institute training faculty that summer.

Stan was also keen to listen to the recordings (with his girlfriend's permission) to see how two REBT therapists would approach the same issue. I, too, was interested in discovering how Ellis and I would approach the session, so I agreed to see the woman and have my session recorded. Ellis also granted permission for his session to be recorded. My session with Susan, and Ellis's session with her with commentary from myself, Hank Robb and John Minor, were published in the *Journal of Rational-*

---

[13] REBT stands for Rational Emotive Behaviour Therapy.

Emotive and Cognitive-Behavior Therapy, 2010, Volume 28, Issue 3.[14]

The transcript of my session with Susan appears below. Please note that I did not know anything about single-session therapy when I conducted the session with Susan. However, I will comment on how I would have intervened differently if a single-session therapy mindset had guided my work.

Susan's Session with Windy Dryden

Windy: OK. So, why don't you start where you want to?

[From an SST perspective, this is not a good way of beginning a single session as it is too broad. For examples of how to begin a single session, see Chapter 5.]

Susan: Well, um, I'm conflicted about … ah, whether or not to live with Stan. I'm married and I have been for 21 years. I just thought I was happily married, until Stan came around, and he kind of got me questioning a lot of things.

Windy: How did he do that?

Susan: Um … just by saying are you happily married? And I said yes. And then … um … just made me think about it. I guess I hadn't thought about it before. But I'm very, very much in love with him and um … he wants me to live with him and I'm conflicted because of my kids.

Windy: How old are your kids?

Susan: I have (teenagers). And conflicted because also

---

[14] The transcript appears with the publisher's kind permission. It was originally published in Dryden (2010).

because my social circle of friends and my kids it all kind of revolves around the religion. And my kids would not ... um ... think it was a very good idea if I was living with somebody.

Windy: Right. Do they know about Stan?

Susan: Mm-hmm.

Windy: What do they think about it?

Susan: Um. They think ... he's the exact opposite of my husband, you know. My husband is very straight, and you can see that Stan is very unconventional. Um. They don't know him. They just have seen him.

Windy: Right. And does your husband know about him?

Susan: Yes.

Windy: And how does he feel about that?

Susan: Um. Well, my husband doesn't like him ... (*laughs*) ... Um and my husband thinks that since Stan is so much the opposite of him that that is like a total rejection of him.

Windy: OK. And how long have you been with Stan?

Susan: Um, about seven months.

Windy: Seven months. Right. And do you see him fairly regularly?

Susan: Mm-hmm. Yeah.

Windy: And he wants to live with you? Does he want to get married to you, or does he just want to live with you?

Susan: Well. He doesn't ... it wouldn't bother him if we didn't get married. But he would marry me. He said he would. But he doesn't think the marriage thing ... it's not that big a deal. Although, he was married for several years, until, um, his wife (had an accident).

Windy: And?

Susan: Died.

Windy: Oh, and died. You seem pretty tearful at the moment.

Susan: Tearful? ...

Windy: Yeah ...

Susan: It's the thought of my kids, you know. Not having anything to do with me. Because of Stan and living with him.

[*My comment about Susan's tearfulness helps us get to identify an important factor.*]

Windy: That's your fear, is it?

Susan: Uh huh.

Windy: So you have a fear that if you went to your kids, and you said, 'Look, I'm going to be living with Stan,' they'll say what?

Susan: They'd probably say, 'Well, you don't have to come around here any more. We don't care to see you.'

Windy: And as you look at that, how? ...

Susan: I mean, it's my whole circle of friends, too. It's all the … religion.

Windy: Right. So, you're not only losing contact with your kids, but you'd be losing the whole contact with the … religion.

Susan: Mm-hmm.

Windy: I don't know much about the … religion. What's…

Susan: It's very strict.

Windy: What's its view on divorce and people living with...?

Susan: They, I mean it's definitely, you don't live with someone unless you're married.

Windy: And knowing your friends in the religion, would they reject you do you think?

Susan: Um, probably. At least to a certain degree.

Windy: Would some reject you more than others?

Susan: Mm-hmm.

Windy: Do you think some of your friends would stand by you?

Susan: Maybe a little bit. But not like, I don't think we would have as close a friendship as I have with them now.

Windy: So, you really do have a lot to lose. What do you have to gain?

Susan: Just Stan and…I don't know. I love him a whole bunch. I don't think I've ever felt like this before about anyone, including my husband. Um, and …

Windy: I noticed before that your face lit up when I asked you that question.

Susan: Mm-hmm.

Windy: Did you notice that?

Susan: I really love him a whole lot. And I…

Windy: How would you feel if you … are you in a situation whereby, it's a situation that you really have to choose either …

Susan: It's going to have to be either/or.

Windy: Yeah. Right.

Susan: I'm pretty darn sure.

Windy: Well. What we do in Rational Emotive Behaviour Therapy in these situations is look at the two poles, the two alternatives, help you to be as clear-headed as you can be about the two, then or even perhaps first, help you over your…any fears that you have about indecisiveness because you've got to…you have a choice to make right? And you're also maybe indecisive. Would you say you are …

              [*Up to now, I have taken care to give Susan space to tell me about the situation she is in so that I can understand the context. I now outline a way forward based on REBT. From an SST perspective, I would have, at the outset, encouraged Susan to set a goal for the session.*]

Susan: Do I have trouble making decisions? Is that what you mean?

Windy: Yeah.

Susan: Um.

Windy: Or just in this area?

Susan: I think just in this area. Pretty much.

Windy: How do you feel about the fact that at the moment you're not able to make a decision that easily? How do you feel about ....

Susan: Well, it's uncomfortable.

Windy: Uh huh. Just uncomfortable or....

Susan: Um. I don't like it.

Windy: Right ... But it sounds as if you're not disturbing yourself about the fact that you are not making a decision ...

[*Here, I am checking to see whether Susan has a secondary emotional problem about her primary emotional problem about not making a decision, which may need to be dealt with first. It appears that she doesn't. This intervention stems from REBT theory. From an SST perspective, I would not have asked this question unless Susan identified it as her nominated problem or there was clear evidence that the existence of this problem would interfere with the work to be done on her nominated problem, if it were different.*]

Susan: Yeah. But I'm going to have to make a decision. I mean, when I go home from here, I'm going to have to make a decision, either move in with Stan, or ...

Windy: Right, so it's as imminent as that?

Susan: Yeah.

Windy: We're talking about over the next few days.

Susan: Yeah.

[*I could have asked why it was so imminent. It transpires that that is part of the problem, as we shall see.*]

Windy: Yeah. Okay. Let's suppose you actually chose to stay with your kids, and the (religious group), you know and stay with your husband. Now, that would mean losing Stan. Right? How would you feel about that?

[*I am setting the pace so far in the session, and she is following my lead. In SST, I would encourage Susan to create a focus, and I would follow her lead.*]

Susan: Devastated.

Windy: Meaning what?

Susan: I don't know. Life wouldn't be too enjoyable I guess.

Windy: Mm-hmm. It wouldn't be enjoyable, but that doesn't equate to being devastated does it? I mean...

Susan: No.

Windy: So, what do you think you've been telling yourself about....

Susan: It would be very hurtful not to have Stan around.

Windy: In what sense?

Susan: Um. He makes me feel very loved.

Windy: So, you would lose something that's very important to you, something you feel loved about, OK? But in our therapy, it's not just that loss that leads to the devastation. It's your attitude towards the loss. Now, what do you think your attitude towards that loss would be?

Susan: Um. I'd be very, very sad.

Windy: But that's healthy because sadness is: 'Look, I'm losing something that's very important to me, that is very sad', *but*, there's always a but here, *but* you know, face it. It's not the end of the world. I would be able to survive and have some happiness, not as much as perhaps, you know, as much as I'd have *with* him, but it wouldn't be the end of the world. Would you say that you were kind of adding that 'it will be the end of the world' aspect to this?

              [*I am using REBT concepts here since it is an REBT session. In SST, I would help Susan to identify times that she dealt with loss healthily and encourage her to use what she was helpful then to her current situation.*]

Susan: Yeah. Probably.

Windy: Now. Would it be the end of the world?

Susan: Well, yeah, it would.

Windy: OK. Are you open to looking at that? OK. Let's suppose ... I give you another scenario, alright. Let's suppose Stan died. OK. Now, do you think you'd ever get over that loss?

Susan: I wouldn't have a choice.

Windy: So...

Susan: I would have to.

Windy: OK. Let's suppose it would be a year after his death. How would you feel?

Susan: I'd probably still be missing him.

Windy: But, where would you be in your life? Would you be missing him and be miserable, you know crying, shutting people away, or would you be starting to regroup and move on?

[Here, I am using the passage of time to help Susan see that she can get over the loss of Stan. This works well in both REBT and SST.]

Susan: I'd probably be regrouping. I guess. I am a survivor.

Windy: OK. Right. You are a survivor. If we bring that into the picture, OK, which said, look, 'If I lost Stan by choosing to go with the (religious group) and my children, that's tremendously sad, *but* it's not the end of the world. I'm a survivor, and I can move on'. Does that kind of bring a different flavour to it or not?

[I am capitalising on one of Susan's strengths – she is a survivor – to help her change her attitude. This is a key intervention in SST.]

Susan: Yeah.

Windy: OK. So now, if you can start to think more rationally, which includes feeling very sad, rational thinking means that you're going to feel very sad about losing Stan. Let's go the other route. Let's suppose you choose Stan. Now, how would you feel about, and let's take the worst, your children say: 'Mum, as far as we are concerned, we have no mother' and the (religious group) say, 'As far as we're concerned, we don't know you.' Now, how would you feel about that?

[I am 'driving the bus here', and Susan is following me. In SST, she would drive the bus, and I would follow her. My basic strategy here is to help Susan approach the loss of Stan, on the one hand, and of her family and friends, on the other, with healthy, flexible and non-extreme attitudes rather than with rigid and extreme attitudes so that she can make a decision free from the influence of the latter. I would take this tack in SST if Susan cannot reference any constructive experiences with loss that we can use. In this case, I would explain my 'take' on her situation and ask her permission to proceed. I do neither here in this session.]

Susan: That would bother me a whole bunch.

Windy: What would the feeling be?

Susan: Mainly my kids.

Windy: OK. Let's stick to the kids. How would you feel about your kids saying that?

Susan: Um. I would feel devastated.

Windy: Again, it's not the loss of the kids, which again is going to feel very, very sad. No, taking away from that, but what would you be adding? What would you bring to that loss that would lead to the devastation?

Susan: That I couldn't stand it.

[Once again, I am using REBT concepts here instead of using Susan's own past success experiences in dealing with loss to help herself now.]

Windy: What couldn't you stand about them saying that?

Susan: Um. I don't know, it's ... they're my kids. You know. I love them.

Windy: Mm-hmm. And therefore....

Susan: I don't want to lose them.

Windy: You don't want to lose them, right, but we have to help you to look at the worst, you know, right in the face. Right? And say, could you tolerate that rejection?

Susan: I could probably tolerate it. But I wouldn't like it.

Windy: That's not your goal. Your goal is not to say 'Hey, my kids rejected me, who cares' or 'My kids have rejected me, I don't mind.' You see. You're going to feel very sad. But the point is our theory says that you're saying something very healthy, which is, 'I've lost something that's very important to me. My kids, they've have rejected me. I can't stand it, and it's terrible.' Now, let me put something to you that you might find strange. Right? Would you leave your kids if it meant it was the only way of keeping them alive?

[Since I have not helped Susan to set a goal for the session, it is wrong of me to tell her what her goal is.]

Susan: Yeah.

Windy: You'd never see them again, but they're alive. Right. How would you feel then?

Susan: If it saved their lives, I would gladly do that.

Windy: But how would you feel about losing them?

Susan: I would be sad.

Windy: So you see what I'm saying here. It's not just the losing them, it's losing them plus the construction, which is 'I couldn't stand it'. But if you couldn't stand it, you'd have to condemn them to death. You see what I'm saying? Let me just see if I'm making myself clear. Can you just run that past me? What do you think I'm saying?

[I am offering Susan a solution based on REBT principles. This is hardly surprising since my brief was to help her with REBT. In SST, she and I would discuss potential solutions and she would select the one that she thinks is best for her.]

Susan: OK. If the only way to keep them alive was to leave them and never see them again, I would gladly do that. Even though I would feel very sad, I would at least know they were okay. They were alive.

Windy: Even though you never saw them again.

Susan: But I could stand that.

Windy: They don't know. They think that you've rejected them. Alright. They don't know…

Susan: Oh, don't! Why'd you throw that in?

Windy: Because it's important, isn't it?

Susan: Yes.

Windy: OK. They think you've rejected them, but you know you're keeping them alive. How would you then feel?

Susan: I guess I could stand that, knowing that it was keeping them alive.

Windy: Right, so, I'm putting this to you. I wonder if your real problem is that you're doing it for you? You're putting you first. Is that an issue for you? I'm putting myself first, my happiness first....

[*If I had asked Susan what her goal was and then what she thought was an obstacle to her reaching that goal, then we may have identified her difficulty with putting herself first earlier.*]

Susan: Probably.

Windy: Is that in there? And how do you feel about that?

Susan: Selfish.

Windy: And what's the feeling that goes along with the selfishness?

Susan: Putting myself down for putting myself first.

Windy: I'm hearing a big 'G'. Do you know what the big 'G' is? Begins with 'G'.

Susan: No.

Windy: You're feeling the <u>guilt</u>.

Susan: Oh! The guilt.

Windy: Is that in there?

Susan: Feeling guilty. Yeah.

Windy: Now, guilt, in Rational Emotive Behaviour Therapy is saying, you're doing the wrong thing, right? I'm a bad person for doing the wrong thing, cos I'm being selfish, right? Is that how you would feel?

   [In SST, I would ask Susan for her understanding of guilt before offering mine.]

Susan: Yeah. Uh-huh.

Windy: Now, how would you be a bad person for doing this, let's suppose, selfish thing?

Susan: Well, I wouldn't be a bad person.

Windy: You wouldn't be a bad person?

Susan: No.

Windy: Why wouldn't you be a bad person?

Susan: I would be happy, but I'd be conflicted still.

Windy: Yeah. Right. And you're going to be conflicted, you see. Now, do you think there may be something here about, 'I really have to make a decision without experiencing the conflicted-ness?' Is that in there at all?

Susan: Um. No, I really don't think so.

Windy: No? It's not in there, OK. So, if I can help you, to first of all take the horror out of losing Stan. Right, and then take the horror out of losing your kids, right, so that you're saying, 'Look, if I lose Stan, that would be very sad, but it's not the end of the world, I can move on. And again, if I lose my kids that would be very bad, but again not the end of the world, I can move on. I would not be a bad person, even if I look at it as if it is selfish.' But selfishness in my book means only putting yourself first and not really giving a damn about other people.

Susan: And so, I do give a damn. Otherwise, I wouldn't be conflicted.

Windy: That's right. Exactly. If you left your kids, it would be because, you are doing it because it would be enlightened self-interest, *but*, and this is a big but, you can't make a decision without feeling that you are breaking some important principle. You can't because you've got the principle of 'I love Stan, I don't want to lose him', and the principle of 'I love my kids, and I don't want to lose them'. You see. So, whatever you do, you're going to break a principle. It's inevitable. You see what I'm saying?

[*In SST, I would check with Susan where we were with her issue and if there was anything we should be discussing that we weren't.*]

Susan: Yeah.

Windy: So, if you accept that then here's what we do. Let's suppose, right – how old are you now?

Susan: Forty-two.

Windy: Right. You're on your deathbed. Right, imagine that. You're on your deathbed. You've stayed with the kids and the (religious group), and you've left Stan. Right. Now. How do you feel about that decision on your deathbed?

Susan: Like I cheated myself.

Windy: You cheated yourself. OK. Now you're on your deathbed, you've gone with Stan, and the worst has happened. The kids have rejected you, and the community's rejected you. Ok. But you're with Stan. How do you feel on your deathbed?

Susan: Is Stan gonna stick around? (*laughs*)

[*This does seem like an important element, which I may have identified earlier if I had asked Susan to specify the crucial factors that related to her decision.*]

Windy: Let's suppose that, because I think that's another element here.

Susan: It is. That's a *big* element.

Windy: We'll come to it in a minute, OK?

Susan: Um.

Windy: How do you feel about it if he stuck around?

Susan: I would feel like I was missing out on a whole world of kids, grandkids, and I missed out.

Windy: Right.

Susan: And so I cheated myself again.

Windy: Right. Which of these two situations would you rather be in? Being on your deathbed, saying, 'I've cheated myself because I've missed out on the only man who I really felt something strongly for.' Or 'I've cheated myself because I've missed out on a whole world of kids, grandkids and the community.' Which of the two situations would you prefer to be in? You've only got one bed! You have to choose.

Susan: That's well, that's kind of my problem.

Windy: I know, but which of the two would you like to....

Susan: I feel that ... oh gosh....

Windy: If you don't choose one of them, there'll be no bed and you're going to burn in hell, so you have to choose. (*Laughs*)

Susan: That's hard ... that's my whole problem. I want it all.

Windy: Right. So we come back to two other issues. Right. Why do you have to have it all?

[*It is clear that Susan is struggling with several elements. From an SST perspective, I would list these two issues and invite her to choose which one she wants to discuss next.*]

Susan: Well, just because I want it. I desire it.

Windy: Alright! And, of course, you run the universe, don't you? I see. OK. Do you have to have it all?

Susan: No.

Windy: Why not?

Susan: I mean, I would survive without having it both ways.

Windy: Right.

Susan: I'm going to have to.

Windy: Right … Let's suppose that we gave you a guarantee that Stan would never leave you. Right. Would that make a difference to you?

Susan: Yeah.

Windy: What difference would it make?

Susan: It would be easier to choose him.

Windy: Yeah. And would you choose him?

Susan: Probably.

Windy: Probably, right. So let's have a look at this other thing. Your fear is, that you choose him, and down the line, what happens?

Susan: He doesn't love me.

Windy: Right.

Susan: And he leaves.

Windy: Right. Now, what do you think you're saying about that?

Susan: I have to have his love, and I don't have to have….

Windy: No, but you're also saying, 'Shit, I've lost Stan and … I've given up my kids.! I'm alone, I've….'

Susan: …lost everything.

Windy: I've lost everything. Right. Now. Is that something that you could live with?

Susan: I could, but it would be very, very difficult. VERY.

Windy: But you could choose him, and he could die.

Susan: I know.

Windy: Because aren't you demanding a guarantee? Aren't you really saying, 'Jesus, if I go with this guy, he has to (a) stay alive, and (b) love me. He's got to promise me this and keep the promise.' Ok. Does he have to do that?

Susan: No.

Windy: Why not?

Susan: Because there are no guarantees. Nobody can guarantee things like that.

Windy: Right. Now let's have a look at a scenario. You've chosen him, he's gone off, he's left you, right. Your kids don't want you back. How would you construct a life for yourself?

Susan: I would have to … um … reach out and meet new people.

Windy: Right. Remember, you're a survivor. Right. How does that seem? It'd be difficult. wouldn't it?

         [*In SST, we take every opportunity to help the clients see how they can use their strengths in dealing with their problems.*]

Susan: I could do it.

Windy: You could do it. Right. So if you take…Let's just go over what we've talked about today. First of all, you need to take the horror out of losing Stan on the one scenario and the horror out of losing the kids. Not the sadness. You will be very sad, whatever you've done. Whatever you decide to do, you're going to be sad. It's important to give up the demand that you have to have it all. And also the demand for a guarantee that if you choose Stan, he's going to stay around and love you.

[In SST, I would ask the client to make such a summary, given that we want to find out what is important to them. Here, my summary indicates what I think is important.]

Susan: Mm-mmh.

Windy: Keep in touch with that image of being a survivor is really important. What do you think about those ideas?

Susan: Yeah. I mean if I can keep that in perspective. I am a survivor. And I'm going to feel sad no matter which way I go. But there are no guarantees my kids are going to be around anyway either. And I mean they're not … they're going to….

Windy: That's right.

Susan: They're going to leave and have their own lives.

Windy: And there's no guarantee that after a while – that you're not going to reform a relationship after they grow up. You don't know that. But we have to deal with the worst you see, because that's what you're thinking about.

Susan: Right.

Windy: Right. So, there are no guarantees. Does that help you in making a decision?

Susan: Yeah.

Windy: In what way?

Susan: I think I'm really going to have to go with Stan.

Windy: OK. But now I'm going to help you to prepare. I'll be the irrational voice and you answer me back. 'You're a selfish woman. What kind of woman would really reject her kids like that?'

[In SST, we encourage the client to rehearse a solution to see how it suits them. I would put what I am doing here under that heading. I am playing devil's advocate so Susan can rehearse the position of deciding to choose Stan.]

Susan: The kind of woman that is really crazy in love with Stan and wants to grab for happiness while she has it available.

Windy: 'But what a selfish person you are. How can you do that? Your poor kids. They need a mother.'

Susan: They've had a mother (into their teenage) years. They've had … I mean, I've been there the whole while.

Windy: Let me play … let's go from a different point of view. 'But how can you trust that man. Look at him! He's a hippy. He's you know … he's …'

Susan: He is that.

Windy: 'You can't trust hippies, you know he might be zooming off. I mean how many other relationships has he had since his wife died?'

Susan: Plenty.

Windy: 'Yeah! How do you know you're not going to be the one that's going to be next on the cast-off list?'

Susan: I don't know. I don't know that.

Windy: 'But you need to know, you need to know, you've gotta know. How could you possibly make a decision without knowing?'

Susan: Well. You have to because there are no guarantees. I mean there are no guarantees. And if I want to grab for this happiness, I have to know that there are no guarantees that he's going to be around. And I can't look back after I do it.

Windy: You can look back, but when you look back ... you see when you look back, you're going to look back by ... it's important to look back in terms of the decisions you've made. So you are going to look back and regret the fact that you've lost your kids and you need to really affirm the reason why you've chosen Stan.

Susan: But there's a lot of negatives that go with choosing Stan too and that's what .... makes the decision....

Windy: What are the negatives?

Susan: Um ... Do we have time?

Windy: I think so.

Susan: He's in debt big time. He is a substance abuser. Big time. Um and he's promised ... he's not on the drug thing, but whenever he gets angry with me he goes back to it.

Windy: So maybe you need to get a commitment from him that so, you know, a commitment that.... Do you really have to make a decision right now? I mean, there's pressure....

Susan: Yeah from Stan.

[*Although I did not say it, I suspect the reason why Stan wanted Susan to have therapy sessions with Albert Ellis and myself was for her to choose him over her family/community.*]

Windy: But why do you have to go along with his pressure?

Susan: I think if I don't make a decision to live with him when I go back home from New York, um, he probably will just say: 'That's it.'

Windy: OK. Now what do you make of that? Here's a man who's in big time debt, and abusing substances, he's asking you to make a damn big commitment *without* making a commitment to you. What commitment would you like from him that would help you to make a decision?

Susan: That he would stay away from abusing drugs and that he will stick around with me.

Windy: Well, why don't you ask for that commitment? But, a commitment of time. That perhaps he's got to be clean for what, how long?

Susan: A year.

Windy: Is he in a treatment programme?

Susan: No. But he....

Windy: Maybe he needs to get into a treatment programme right?

Susan: Well, but he does that.

Windy: He's in a treatment programme but he still abuses?

Susan: No, he runs, he does the Rational....

Windy: Who cares? He still ... he's still abusing substances. Now my point is to you, he's asking you to make a commitment, a big commitment to leave your kids. Don't you also have the right to actually ask for something from him?

Susan: I would say I do, but then we just did this great big talk with ... nobody has any rights.

Windy: I'm not talking about rights in the absolute sense, I'm talking about rights in the sensible sense.

Susan: Since he's asking me to make a commitment I can feel okay with asking him to make a commitment.

Windy: Yeah. It's a commitment in ... I mean if you were ... if I was in this situation with you and you were ... I would say to you, 'I need to know that you're going to be off these blasted drugs for a decent amount of time, and that the first time that we have an argument, you're not going to rush back and take the drugs. I don't need to know... but this is my bottom line, hadn't you better ask yourself, what kind of commitment am I going to be asking from him to do before I make this leap.

Susan: Mm-hmm. That's a very, very good ... idea. *Very* good.

[Right at the end of the session, we seemed to have identified the most important issue. Stan is asking Susan to make a life-changing decision without being prepared to commit to anything in return. And, most importantly, it had not occurred to Susan that she could ask Stan for such a commitment. I wonder if I had approached the session with an SST mindset if I would have identified this central issue earlier in the session.]

Windy: OK.

Susan: Very good. I feel really good about that.

[Susan's response indicates that this is the central issue for which she has a solution.]

Windy: OK. But don't forget the other stuff, because when you go back, and actually make a decision, let's suppose he's clean for a year, he could still go off and have the drugs a day after you go with him. You need to be prepared for that. You need to deal with all these other issues we're talking about. But it seems to me as if you are willing to give up a whole big life to a man who takes substances, you know, as soon as he gets angry. You see.

[I thought it important to remind Susan of the issues we covered even though the issue of asking Stan for a commitment seems to be the most important for her.]

Susan: Uh-huh.

Windy: Now, you know ... I mean....

Susan: And he is in debt big time, and my husband ... you know ... has got a fair amount of money.

Windy: Yeah, exactly.

Susan: That's another big thing.

Windy: Maybe you also need to ask him … that again, the other thing is that maybe I need to see evidence that you are being more responsible with your money. Is living with somebody who's responsible important to you?

Susan: Yeah I think so.

                 The tape cuts out here.

Reflections

As the session unfolded, I identified and discussed several emotional problems that Susan had, which underpinned her difficulty with decision-making. These were as follows:

- Her anxiety about losing her kids, friends and community if she chose Stan;
- Her anxiety about her kids thinking that she had rejected them if she chose Stan and the guilt she would experience if they thought this;
- Her anxiety about losing Stan if she chose her current life situation;
- Her feelings of guilt about acting selfishly;
- Her reluctance to choose Stan because she thinks she needs a guarantee that he would not reject her later if she chose him;
- Her reluctance to make a decision because doing so means losing something important when she holds that she must have it all;
- Her view that she needs to make a quick decision in response to Stan's pressure.

The Dilemma of Being Comprehensive vs Being Focused

I do some work on all of the above-mentioned issues, but I tend to switch from problem to problem as Susan discloses them. At that time, before I developed my interest and skill in single-session therapy, I believed that in single sessions, when the situation is complex, the therapist is faced with the choice of being comprehensive and spending some time on all revealed emotional problems or focusing on one major problem to the exclusion of all else. In my session with Susan, I chose the former tack but wonder what the outcome would have been if I chose the latter. Thus, in hindsight, I could have asked Susan, 'Which one issue shall we focus on, the resolution of which would help you make a decision?' This would have given the session a greater focus and may have facilitated Susan's decision-making.

How I Would Have Conducted the Session with Susan if I Had Adopted a Single-Session Therapy Mindset

In my comments on my session with Susan, I pointed out in several places how I would have intervened differently if I had brought a single-session therapy mindset to the session rather than an REBT mindset. Let me summarise how I would have intervened differently with Susan if I had held an SST mindset.

- I would have clarified with Susan at the very outset what she thought the purpose of our session was.
- I would have asked her for her session goal.
- I would have worked with her to create a focus for the session. This would probably have related to the major obstacle to her making a decision.
- I would have asked her if she had faced a similar decision in the past and how she made this decision. I would have encouraged her to draw upon the factors that helped her make this decision.
- I would have elicited her strengths as a person in addition to her being 'a survivor', which we identified in the session. I would have then encouraged her to make use

of these strengths as appropriate.

- I would have worked with her to identify a solution that would have helped her make a decision and rehearse this solution. I did this in the session when I encouraged her to lay down healthy boundaries with Stan.
- I would have asked her to summarise what we had discussed.

The tape then cut out, so I am not sure what happened after this, but I am sure that I did not do the following, which I would have done if I were guided by the SST mindset.

- I would have asked what she would take away from the session.
- Before we finished, I would have encouraged her to tell me anything or ask me anything about the issue that she would regret not telling me or asking me, thus bringing the session to a good conclusion.

As with other single sessions, I do not know what happened to Susan after our session or what decision she made.

See Chapter 7 for a discussion of how I have integrated REBT into SST.

3

A Demonstration Session of REBT with a Man Seeking Help for a Procrastination Problem (2008)

Preamble

The Albert Ellis Institute has a Master Therapist DVD series showcasing the work of different REBT therapists working with an actual client on the client's nominated problem. I participated in this series in 2008 and saw a young man (whom I will call 'Monty') seeking help for his procrastination problem. (Dryden, 2008).[15] The client was an actor but was asked to present a real problem he had and wanted help with. As with the session I did with 'Susan', which appears in Chapter 2, the session I did with Monty is a single session since it was agreed that we would only meet for one time. As with the session that I did with 'Susan' I did not approach the work from a single-session therapy mindset since I had not incorporated this way of thinking in any of my work at that time. However, my work shows how I approached a single session of REBT at that time. The ongoing comments of the demonstration session are like those that I made of my session with Susan, based on what I would have done if I had approached the session while holding an SST mindset.

---

[15] The transcript was originally published in Dryden (2012) and appears here with the kind permission of the publisher.

Monty's Session with Windy Dryden

Windy: Hello, Monty, thank you for coming in today. What problem would you like to present today?

               [*From the outset, I adopt a problem focus which is consistent with both SST and REBT.*]

Monty: Er, procrastination, very long term and sometimes large scale.

Windy: How do you define procrastination to yourself?

               [*In SST, it is vital that the client and therapist 'speak the same language'. As it is easy for two people to use a term like 'procrastination' in different ways, I ask Monty how he uses the term.*]

Monty: Well, it's putting off things that … putting off the thing, and this is just sort of putting off critical things, it's a sort of a total problem, putting off things till the last minute or past the last minute that I have plenty of time to take care of that leads me into being like chronically late for things, chronically like stressing out about something that has been on the plate for a long time and, yeah, sort of like creating massive problems for myself that didn't have to exist.

Windy: Yeah, I have a slightly different definition of procrastination. I see procrastination as putting off a task that is in your interest to do and putting it off beyond the time when it's in your interest to do it.

Monty: I like that definition.

Windy: Yeah?

Monty: I think that sounds like what I'm talking about.

[*We agree to use my definition of procrastination so that we have a shared view of the problem under consideration (Dryden, 2011).*]

Windy: So maybe take an example of ... maybe a current example, maybe a typical example ... of a task that you're putting off doing that it would be in your interest to do at a time when it would be in your interest to do it.

[*As is typical in both SST and REBT I ask Monty for a specific example of his procrastination problem.*]

Monty: Sure, like in the last twenty-four hours, there are two examples. One is I was supposed to have like the treatment of a script ready by the close of last week, there's a cast waiting on it, there's a pay cheque waiting on it ... had a lot of time. The script is not finished, the treatment is not in and it was one of these things where I was moving up to start another project out of State recently and there were a few days before going up that I had kind of in my mind that I'm going to take care of this, it's going to be, you know, I should have enough hours to take care of it and it won't get....

Windy: So it would be useful to focus on that particular episode ... you mentioned two?

Monty: Yeah, I was about to say the other one is a more general situation which sort of pops up continuously which is....

Windy: Which would be more meaningful for you to focus on?

Monty: Umm, yeah, actually now that I think about it, maybe the sort of the systemic as opposed to ... the script is sort of a specific anomalous thing while the other thing I was thinking about is something that kind of comes up.

Windy: I still would like to take an example, if we go with the second one....

Monty: Sure.

Windy: ... I'll be asking you for an example.

[Monty provides two examples, so to strengthen the working alliance between us I ask him to choose one of the two (Bordin, 1979). However, I stress the importance of Monty selecting a specific example of the problem whichever one he chooses.]

Monty: Oh yeah, I've got this. It's most recent but it's part of a long and endless system.

Windy: So do you want to go with the systemic one and take an example of that?

Monty: Yeah. This is like ... as an actor pretty much everything is ... everything is time sensitive, like extremely time sensitive, and just recently, again, it's the most recent example is there is like a theatre company that I did some work with sort of by accident very recently and the Artistic Director and everything was like 'great job', we need you to send in your headshot and all of the standard actor stuff, and ... did not do it.

Windy: It is still something that you're putting off?

Monty: It's still something I'm putting off.

Windy: OK, so....

Monty   It's like, I mean, I could have done it yesterday before coming here.

Windy: Can I ask you then ... if I were to ask you to define a time where you would agree with yourself, perhaps later on today, that you're going to sit down and do this task and yet you suspect that at that time you might put it off even having made that agreement with yourself, when might that be, would it be later on today?

[Here I assume that Monty has a goal with respect to this task. From an SST perspective, I would not have made this assumption. I would have asked Monty for his goal.]

Monty: It would be like later on today.

Windy: What time would you say?

Monty: Like, you know, 3.00 pm.

[As in REBT, the SST therapist can maximise their impact with the client if they help the client select a specific example of their problem that is imminent with a specified starting time. This helps both assessment and intervention and additionally provides the client with an immediate opportunity to deal constructively with his problem.]

Windy: So let's take 3.00 pm, let's take 3.00 pm and what I want to do is to try and get a flavour of how you procrastinate. So you have agreed with yourself, right....

Monty: Yeah.

Windy: ... you're going to do this task, and the task involves what, by the way?

Monty: Yeah, getting to the computer, printing out a cover letter....

Windy: OK, so come three o'clock you have an agreement with yourself, you're going to sit down on this computer and get this cover letter done ... and yet you are beginning to procrastinate. Can you imagine really focusing on that as a situation?

Monty: Absolutely.

Windy: Now, what do you think is going on at that point, what would it ... what do you think might be going through your mind at that point that might lead you to break that agreement with yourself?

[I am guided by REBT theory here. From an SST perspective, I might have asked Monty for his explanation of the barrier to starting the work at 3 pm.]

Monty: At some level there is a 'ooh, I've got a little bit more time' so there are some other things that I could sneak in there. But there's also like a certain level of ... I mean, it's, it's like a, like I don't want to have to do it at that time.

Windy: You don't want to have to do it at that time, right.

Monty: If that makes any sense....

Windy: So the first one it sounds like you're beginning to kind of create a story which would....

Monty: Justify why....

Windy: ... justify and that's what we call a rationalisation.

Monty: I'm good at those.

Windy: You're good at those?

Monty: Yeah.

Windy: OK, and the other one, it sounds like you're beginning to experience some emotion which you are then moving away from. Would you say that would be correct?

[Monty's response indicates that he would rationalise not beginning the task ('I've got a little more time...') and that his procrastination would be motivated by an avoidance of feeling. I acknowledge both but decide to assess the avoided feeling. From an SST perspective, I would ask Monty to select which element he deemed more important in dealing with his procrastination. decide which element.]

Monty: Yeah.

Windy: What do you think that emotion would be, that if you really allowed yourself to feel it that you might experience?

Monty: It's like it's something like a, it's like a fear or something but it's....

Windy: Fear?

Monty: Yeah, it's the first word that comes to mind but it's...

Windy: I'll tell you what the first word that came to my mind when I was listening to you and, listen, the point of this is that I may very well be wrong...

Monty: Yeah.

Windy: ... OK, and correct me if I'm wrong, but I kind of got a sense that you might be starting to feel, if you actually started to kind of do it, some kind of anger or resentment?

Monty: Yeah, that's resentment towards it.

Windy: Resentment?

Monty: Yeah, absolutely.

Windy: Right.

[*Here, I asked Monty what he would feel if he allowed himself to stay with the task and not procrastinate and he says 'fear'. However, he says it in such a tentative way, and his response seems to be at variance with what he said earlier (i.e. 'I don't want to have to do it at that time') that I put forward an alternative emotion that more likely goes along with the sense of doing something that he does not want to do, i.e. 'resentment' which Monty resonates with better than with 'fear'. At this point in the session, I was looking for consistency between the language that he used and the feeling that he came up with and I did not find such consistency. In putting forward my hypothesis about his emotion, I was careful to give him the opportunity to disconfirm my hypothesis by saying 'correct me if I'm wrong'. What I did here is consistent with REBT. From an SST perspective, I would have first seen if Monty had successful experiences in dealing with his procrastination issue in the past and if so, I would have encouraged him to bring these experiences to his current issue. If not, I would have asked Monty if he was interested in my take on what he was saying and if he was, I would then have intervened in the same as I did in the session.*]

Windy: Can you see that that resentment is somehow connected to your procrastination?

Monty: Yeah.

Windy: In what way would you say?

Monty: I mean, it's a ... I mean the worst part of this is to having to slog through like endless amounts of outreach letters.

Windy: Even though it's in your interest?

Monty: Even though ... I mean, because even though you know it's part of the ... it's like that's not ... like I don't think anybody gets into any of the creative fields, acting especially, like looking forward to do a whole lot of like outreach letters. I mean, even in spite of the fact that it's very clearly connected to the thing, I mean it's, yeah.

Windy: You mentioned fear and I kind of noticed resentment. What do you think that in this episode that you're talking about, three o'clock, do you think the fear is the feeling that's going to stop you or the resentment?

Monty: It's the resentment.

Windy: It's the resentment, OK. Who or what are you resentful towards? Is it a person, is it you, is it life conditions or ... what's the object of your resentment?

[*Having agreed that resentment is Monty's avoided emotion, I begin the search for what he is resentful towards. From an SST perspective, I would have first explained what I was planning to do – understand his resentment better using ideas from REBT – before proceeding with his agreement.*]

Monty: That's a good question and the general result is that I get angry at myself for procrastinating that's the immediate after effect.

[*This is an important choice point in the session. In response to my question concerning the object of his resentment, Monty responds by providing a secondary problem (anger at himself for procrastinating). While REBT encourages therapists to look for and work with such problems when these interfere with work on the primary problem, it would have been a mistake for me to have done this. Working on the secondary problem may be colluding with the client's own tendency to put off dealing with his primary procrastination problem. Also, by changing the focus at this point, I would be providing a poor role model for Monty who shifts focus both in the session and when there is a task to be done. This 'shifting focus' is characteristic of those who have a chronic problem with procrastination and the therapist should endeavour to model 'retaining the focus' for the client. These points are also consistent with SST. By now I would have agreed a focus with Monty – to address his procrastination issue – and when he brought up this secondary problem, I would have encouraged him to remain with the agreed focus, unless he thought that this secondary issue was more important to him.*]

Windy: Well, listen, if we went with that we'd be putting off dealing with the problem.

Monty: (*laughter*) I know that.

Windy: Sure.

Monty: I mean, I think that the resentment is... I think it's definitely targeted at the, I don't know, the sort of the ... the ... I mean, not the specific people that I'm sending it to.

Windy: It's not...?

Monty: I mean, it's not like I think of like the Artistic Director who gave me the job the other day and was like sending in some extra work. It's not like specifically like how can you make me send this in, it's more like I just wish that wasn't the case that I have.

Windy: Yeah.

Monty: You know, I guess it's one of those things like you must do this and not only must I do this on this day, but you have to send in the head shots, the agents who aren't going to look at the thing, there's like a general level.

Windy: So it kind of sounds that you're experiencing and, again, correct me if I'm wrong, that somehow you are in a situation where your freedom is being curtailed.

Monty: Definitely.

Windy: Yeah?

Monty: Definitely.

Windy: And would you say that you are angry about being put in that situation?

Monty: Definitely.

               [*Here, I have assessed what Monty is resentful
               about which is 'I am being put in a situation that
               curtails my freedom.' In SST, I strive to get to the
               heart of the matter and I feel like I am doing just
               that at this juncture.*]

Windy: So what do you do to prove that you are a free man
               at that time?

Monty: I will like play video games.

Windy: Right, OK. 'I'm a free man!'

Monty: And pretty much anything that I can find, at the
               lowest level. It's like when I'm at the computer and
               like Word is open, it can be like turn on some kind
               of –

Windy: Yeah, so somehow, as long as you are kind of
               resentful about having your freedom curtailed and
               you are in a situation, you're going to prove to
               yourself that you are a free man, you are going to
               continue to procrastinate. Is that correct?

Monty: That sounds spot on.

               [*Here I help Monty to see that from his perspective
               engaging in non-task behaviour helps him to restore
               his sense of freedom at that time, which he later
               calls 'Monty time'.*]

Windy: OK, so what would you like to do instead?

Monty: At?

Windy: At three o'clock.

Monty: Like today?

Windy: Yeah.

Monty: That's a good question, rather than writing this up?

Windy: No, I mean....

Monty: I would really like to get the letter out of the way....

Windy: Yeah.

Monty: ... that's, I mean, I'd like it to be gotten out of the way because that's the thing that like, I would really like to work with this company in the future and –

Windy: Can I just feed back something to you about your language?

Monty: Yeah, you don't like the way [*laughs*].

Windy: Well, 'I'd like it to be gotten out of the way, rather than you doing it' [*laughs*]. Well, let's face it, you're not going to like to do it....

Monty: No.

Windy: ... but would it be more accurate to say well look, I'm going to choose to do it even though I don't want to do it because I want the outcome?

[In this section, I address the issue of goals with Monty. From an SST perspective, I could have done this in a clearer way. I also give him feedback about his use of passive language: 'I'd like it gotten out of the way.' Instead, I emphasise the active, choice-based nature of his engaging with the task instead of procrastinating: 'I'm going to choose to do it even though I don't want to do it because I want the

outcome. From an SST perspective, I could have contrasted these two stances, asked him which one would most likely help him to achieve his goal and dealt with any doubts, reservations and objections that he might have about his chosen stance.]

Monty: Yeah.

Windy: OK. Now, in order to do that I guess we're going to have to help you to have a different attitude towards having your freedom curtailed. Because, you see, it sounds like, you know, I mean, I personally don't like having my freedom curtailed and yet I actually don't procrastinate that much because while we are grappling with the same issue here, I have an attitude that states that while I don't like having my freedom curtailed, I don't have to be exempt from that. I can actually choose to do something that I don't want to do to get the result I do want to want and in a funny sense I'm actually freer because in a strange sense it sounds like you have to do the video games to prove how free you are. And that's a bit of a dilemma because when you say you have to you are not free....

[*REBT basically provides clients with an attitudinal solution to emotional and behavioural issues, which I outline here to Monty. After all, I am demonstrating REBT. From an SST perspective, there are several different solutions that Monty could select from depending on his past effective experiences of dealing with procrastination and what internal and external resources he could bring to address the issue. If he brought little to the table, I would ask him if he would be interested in hearing my 'take' on how he could address his problem. If he were interested, I would outline an attitudinal solution as I did above and see what he thought of it.*]

Monty: Yeah [*laughs*]. Ah bright light of day.

Windy: Oh yeah bright light of day. Exactly. Well, look, I reckon that there are three possible attitudes you can have towards having your freedom curtailed and let's have a look at them and let's have a look at the consequences of them and let's have a look at what's in your interest and let's have a look at... and then we can examine them.

The first one, and this is going to sound a bit strange but it's a theoretical possibility, but it does involve you lying to yourself, and that is the idea of what we call indifference and that would go something like this. 'I don't care one way or the other whether my freedom is being curtailed or no. It is a matter of indifference to me.'

Now, is that kind of something that appeals to you?

Monty: I am not ... I mean, it's definitely like it's an active, like I am gonna to do something that is my choice.

Windy: I'm going to do something that is my choice because I have to prove what?

Monty: I don't know if it's ... I don't know if these are the thoughts of I've got to prove something. I don't know, maybe that is ... it is definitely like, and this extends into a lot of different areas, but if there's definitely one thing it's like I just need to go to ground for a second....

Windy: You need to go to ground?

Monty: Go to ground as in like I need to go and just have Monty time and like not ... even though Monty time includes specifically not doing the things that I need to do.

Windy: Monty time is in your mind, free time?

Monty: It's my brain's sort of interpretation of like personal freedom.

Windy: Yeah, so it's like a positive, yeah. So let's come back to the other two possible attitudes that you can have towards the curtailment of freedom is this, look, 'I must not have my freedom curtailed, I really must not' or 'I don't like it if my freedom is curtailed but, sadly and regretfully, that doesn't mean I'm exempt from that.'

Now, which do you think you implicitly believe that leads to your resentment and procrastination?

[Here, I more formally present the REBT model of resentment-based procrastination by outlining the three possible attitudes Monty could hold in this situation with respect to having his freedom curtailed: an indifference attitude, a rigid attitude or a flexible attitude. I then ask him which attitude underpins his resentment/procrastination. This approach is known as the theory-driven approach to REBT assessment (DiGiuseppe, 1991). From an SST perspective, I would do precisely the same once Monty had given me the green light to proceed with an attitudinal solution.]

Monty: I mean, on an emotional level, definitely A.

Windy: Where it is a must?

Monty: Yeah.

Windy: OK.

Monty: I understand that I really need to do these things but I feel that I should really, you know, take them on and do something....

Windy: But as long as you believe, or act as if you believe, because in a way you never actually get to... you see, the thing about procrastination is it's basically a problem of avoidance, right, and therefore what you are avoiding is dealing with the issue of having your freedom curtailed.

You never get there. But, even though you never get there, you are reinforcing through your behaviour the idea that you have to have your freedom at that time. Your behaviour is strengthening the very attitude that is leading to your procrastination.

Monty: Yeah, I'll buy that.

[Monty can see that his rigid attitude underpins his procrastination. I capitalise on this by showing him that his procrastination also reinforces this rigid attitude.]

Windy: Yeah, OK. So the other alternative is to say well look, 'I don't like having my freedom curtailed, but sadly and regretfully, I don't have to be immune from it or exempt from it and, therefore, I can choose to do what I don't want to do to get the results that I do want to have.'

And I put that to you, Monty, that that is true freedom. I put that to you that what you're doing is that you are a prisoner of your own must and musts don't give you freedom to manoeuvre. So when you think you're free, you're really a prisoner of your own musts.

What do you think of that idea?

Monty: I think it seems to hold water.

[From both an REBT perspective and an SST perspective, I could have achieved the same outcome by asking Monty questions rather than making declarative statements.]

Windy: OK, so let's see if we can't rewind and put it into a situation that we will actually have at three o'clock, right? Typically speaking, what will happen today at three o'clock, your motivation would be to have this thing out of the way, right?

Monty: Correct.

Windy: So presumably, if a little fairy came along and did it for you, you would not object?

Monty: Absolutely not. I spend a lot of time thinking that.

Windy: OK, so typically you are acting on the attitude, 'Oh, I'm being made to do something which I see is a curtailment of my freedom. I must not have this curtailment, I'm going to prove that I'm a free man, I'm going to have Monty time, I'm going to do what I want to do, prove I've got a free mind.' If you act out what you normally do, that would happen, is that correct?

Monty: Yeah.

Windy: OK. So let's go back, let's really focus on this one. I'm going to play the must, right, and let's see if you can answer it back and see where we go.

Monty: OK.

Windy: It's three o'clock and I'm ... it's a bit like when you see the Mickey Mouse and Donald Duck, I'm going to be the little Monty devil.

Monty: Nice idea [*laughs*].

Windy: Monty, listen, your freedom is being curtailed, you know, that mustn't happen to you, you need Monty time. Now, how are you going to respond to that?

Monty: That Monty time will be richer in the future if I have Monty time on stage.

Windy: Yeah, but 'I must not really have this curtailment now, I've got to get rid of this negative thing right now.'

Monty: Bear with me, we'll take care of this and there will be Monty time later.

Windy: Yeah, but, Monty, how are you going to ... what attitude are you going to take to this curtailment of your freedom?

Monty: I'd suck it up, I guess.

Windy: Suck it up?

Monty: Yeah.

Windy: Which means what?

Monty: Just....

Windy: I'm a poor British....

Monty: Yeah, let's say that's Americanese for take it on the chin, keep on....

Windy: Take it on the chin?

Monty: Keep on going.

Windy: What attitude towards the curtailment of freedom does that represent?

Monty: Again, it's not a constructive attitude.

Windy: Isn't it?

Monty: No.

Windy: OK, so....

Monty: It's not the choice and I guess the choice is, again, as you've said, it's just like this is the choice that....

Windy: Yeah.

Monty: ... like Monty time is creating the present and future for myself in which success in my craft which leads very obviously to personal happiness for myself and my loved ones is the priority as opposed to like immediate....

Windy: But let's kind of really zero in on the attitude, lets have a look at those two attitudes ... we are going to ditch the indifference belief.

Monty: Yeah.

Windy: Let me go over them and have them side by side. The first one is saying 'I ... OK, my freedom is being curtailed, I must have freedom, I can't bear to have this curtailed.'

                [From an SST perspective, I would have given a clear explanation of my strategy, which is to help him examine his attitudes and asked for his permission to proceed with it before doing so.]

Monty: Right.

Windy: As opposed to look, 'I don't like this but I don't have to be exempt from it, it's bearable, I can tolerate it and it's worth it.'

Monty: Yeah.

Windy: Which of those attitudes is true and which is false? Is there a law which says that Monty must be free…?

Monty: Free now, not so much. I mean, like, I don't know, it's at the point … at a certain level where it's like I remember having that time or something and maybe like it's a, yeah, and I don't know if I have ever read a law that says there has to be.

Windy: No, exactly.

Monty: Well, even if there was an unspoken law it's like–

Windy: Actually, paradoxically, if there was a law you couldn't go against it. You'd be a prisoner of it.

Monty: There it is.

Windy: That's it and that's the ironic thing, because when you are a prisoner you're not free. You're not free to choose at the moment when your attitude is 'I've got to get rid of this state of affairs right now where I am faced with doing something that I don't want to do even though it is in my interest to do it'.

So … but is it true, let's break it down, is it true that you would, at the time when your freedom is being curtailed is it true that you don't like that?

Monty: Yeah.

Windy: OK, and is it also true 'but there's no reason why I have to be exempt from that'?

Monty: That's also true.

Windy: OK, so if you put that together it would be look, 'I don't like this but I don't have to be exempt from it, it's true and the idea that I must be exempt from it,

I must get rid of it, I must not be, you know, have my freedom curtailed, that's not true.' Which of those two is healthier for Monty?

Monty: I mean, it's definitely choosing to go non-exempt.

Windy: OK, which would you like to commit yourself to working on at three o'clock?

Monty: Definitely the choice of not being exempt.

Windy: Right, but now we're going to have to deal with one other issue which I think is in there and that is, when you make that choice you're going to be uncomfortable.

[From an SST perspective, I am leading the session at this point rather than working in tandem with Monty. I am assuming that dealing with discomfort will be an issue for Monty rather than asking him whether it would be or not.]

Monty: Yeah.

Windy: Do you know why?

Monty: Because it's a change from the norm.

Windy: Because there's freedom over here, there's videos over here which is Monty time and over there there's doing what you don't want to do even though it's in your interest. So you're actually going to feel uncomfortable because you've chosen to do what you don't want to do when there's an option of doing what you do want to do, right?

Monty: Yeah.

Windy: Right, so, I guess, what would you typically say about that discomfort that might lead you to go to the video games, what attitude do you think you might be acting on, the idea that I've got to get rid of it or –

Monty: I mean, absolutely. It's definitely the thing like I'll be working on the thing for real and be like man, this is like what a pain in the ass and then I will just temporarily just jump in here for a second so that I can feel like I'm having some of my time and then come back.

Windy: Well, you see, you could still say this is a pain in the ass and still stick with it.

Monty: Right.

Windy: But in order to do that you have to see that again you have a rigid idea about lack of freedom because you're telling yourself, I'm hearing, I've got to get rid of this discomfort right now. Oh look, there's a very good way of doing it.

Monty: Yeah, the click.

Windy: The click, as opposed to, let's be honest, 'I'm uncomfortable right now but I don't have to be free of that, I can tolerate the discomfort and see what happens' you see?

So I would suggest perhaps a little homework assignment, we kind of suggest these things, and it would be at three o'clock, right, recognise that you made like a contract with yourself, right, recognise that when you sit down, you are going to have an urge, and it could be backed up by rationalisation, oh I've had a hard time, you know, things like that or even Professor Dryden is making me do it which I'm not, it's just a suggestion.

So at that point you can either choose, and I'd suggest that you can rehearse this in your mind, 'I don't like this curtailment feeling, I don't like this discomfort but I'm going to stick with it, it's in my interests. I don't have to be free right now in the way that I want freedom but I can have true freedom and choose to do something that I don't want to do when it's in my interest to do that because when I am going to the video games I'm not free because I believe I have to get rid of these other things.'

[In the above part of the session, I am working with Monty on his attitude to discomfort. While people procrastinate for different reasons, most clients with a chronic procrastination problem have great difficulty engaging with a task when they feel uncomfortable. So, I bring up the topic of handling discomfort with Monty even though he has not explicitly mentioned it. I would go as far as to say that if REBT therapists do not help their procrastinating clients to develop an attitude of discomfort tolerance, then these clients will be particularly vulnerable to relapse. However, from an SST perspective, I might have decided not to raise this issue if Monty did not think he needed to deal with it. While I would have been conflicted about this, I would share these two views and let Monty choose the path forward on this matter.

As this was an REBT demonstration session, I negotiated a specific homework assignment with Monty. People who procrastinate need a clear marker for when they are procrastinating. So Monty knows that he will procrastinate if he does not begin work by 3 pm that afternoon. I have found that the more specific clients can be with themselves regarding when they are going to do something and in which context, the more likely they will do it. Also, I think that the sooner after the session clients agree to carry out a negotiated homework assignment, the more likely again they are to do it.

From an SST perspective, I would have worked with Monty to develop a more general solution to his issue with a corresponding action plan. Then I would have negotiated the same specific assignment to 'kick-off' the change process with the specific situation I was discussing in the session with Monty.]

Windy: Now, can you imagine doing that?

[From an SST perspective I am encouraging Monty to rehearse the attitudinal solution.]

Monty: Yeah.

Windy: OK, now imagine you're doing that and imagine you've started to type, what happens then?

Monty: I mean, even now just thinking about it, I can … like the images of like, man, but that game is right there.

Windy: OK.

Monty: Immediately popping up.

Windy: OK, fine. That's fine. That's realistic and there's nothing that I can do or say that's going to stop you from having that thought pop up in your mind. Now, the question is, how are you going to respond to that thought?

Monty: The response to the thought is yes, there's the thought but here's the thing. I mean, it's definitely true in personal experience that like when I succeed in pushing through like projects, be they late or whatever, it's always the feeling is a thousand times better than any, you know, temporary like stop gap.

Windy: But it sounds like at that point, you see, having ... it's almost like you back yourself into a corner and there's nowhere for you to go, that's what happens when you come at the last minute.

Monty: Yeah.

[*From an REBT perspective, I missed an opportunity to help Monty develop and rehearse a flexible attitude concerning dealing with the immediate lure of the video game.*]

Windy: Do you also have a sense that, in a way, you work better under pressure at the last minute?

[*From an SST perspective, I am again leading too much. However, I have helped Monty to identify a justification for continued procrastination. Note below how I suggest that he needs to test this hypothesis rather than assume that this is true.*]

Monty: Absolutely.

Windy: Yeah.

Monty: That's definitely....

Windy: How do you know that since you haven't tested that? [*laughs*].

Monty: [*laughs*] Because that is generally the way I work.

Windy: Must be good because I do it [*laughs*].

Monty: I'm not sure what you mean [*laughs*].

Windy: The point is you may well be right but you can experiment so the question is, let's just come back to that thought. 'Yes, there's a video game in here and the response towards that is "Yes, there is!" But what am I going to choose to do?'

Monty: Let's leave it there.

Windy: 'Yeah, OK, and I don't want to do it but I want....'

Monty: I want it done.

Windy: 'I want it done and since....' I suppose you could get somebody to do it for you but that's not going to be....

Monty: Not at this level.

Windy: Not at this level. So is that a realistic image, that you are now at your desk. At what point do you think ... is there a slight over the hump, that after a while once you get into it you'll get into the letter?

Monty: Absolutely.

Windy: Yeah.

Monty: There's even like periods of time where I'm sort of easier on....

Windy: You see, I often find that. It's really ... it's like getting over the hump....

Monty: Yeah.

Windy: ... when you ... first of all, you know, what happens typically in your case is you approach the task, as you approach in your mind, curtailment of freedom, I've got to get rid of that, I need Monty time, rationalisation, OK. You've got you through that and then you've started to do it and then there's still a part of your mind that says hey....

Monty: Right.

Windy: Yeah, there is, OK. Now, as you get into it the chances are you might still get those thoughts but the more you get into it they probably will lessen.

Monty: Yeah.

Windy: Alright. Now, what about trying that... well, actively committing yourself to do that at three o'clock this afternoon?

Monty: Absolutely.

Windy: OK, it would be very interesting to see what happens to you.

Monty: OK, thanks a lot.

Windy: Thank you.

[From an SST perspective, I did not do the following:

- *I did not ask Monty to summarise what we covered.*
- *I did not ask him for his takeaways.*
- *I did not ask him if he wanted to tell me or ask me anything before we finished that he might have wanted to tell me or ask me when he reflected on the session later.]*

As this was a one-off demonstration session showing how an REBT therapist endeavoured to help someone who has a procrastination problem, I do not know what use Monty made of the session in his life. What I do know is that the session differed in several respects from an SST session, as I made clear in the comments that I made throughout the transcript. Also, see Chapter 7 in this volume for a discussion of how REBT can be integrated into SST.

4

A Demonstration Session of SST with a Woman Seeking Help for a Procrastination Problem (2024)

Preamble

As I mentioned in the Preface to this book, I have carried out many live demonstration sessions of therapy over the years. In Chapter 3, I presented a discussion from an SST perspective of a demonstration session I did in 2008 of REBT. I included that session here to show how I approached conducting a demonstration session of REBT without the benefit of holding a single-session therapy mindset. A collection of my work showing my development as an SST therapist would not be complete, in my view, without me showing how I currently approach a demonstration session of SST. Consequently, in this chapter, I present the transcript of a demonstration session that I did with Sarah[16] on 29 January 2024, as part of a workshop on 'Writing Procrastination' that I did for Onlinevents. The session was conducted over Zoom in front of a live audience of therapists who signed up for this event. My ongoing comments on this session are based on my holding an SST mindset. I have also included, with her permission, Sarah's commentary on the session.

I have chosen to include this particular session here so that you can compare this session (conducted in 2024) with the session that appears in Chapter 3 (conducted in 2008).

---

[16] A pseudonym. Sarah has kindly given me permission to include the transcript here. The interview lasted for 31 minutes, 34 seconds.

Sarah's Session with Windy Dryden

Windy: Good evening, Sarah. How are you?

Sarah: Hi Windy. I'm well, thank you.

Windy: That's good. So, from your perspective, what's your understanding of the purpose of our conversation this evening?

[WD: *This is how I typically begin any SST session. It is vital that Sarah and I have the same intention for the session.*]

Sarah: For me to explain about my problems around procrastination, help me maybe focus in on something, because it's more than one thing, and hopefully have a takeaway that I can action and get a bit of movement where I've been feeling stuck.

Windy: OK. So tell me what you think I need to know in order for us to have a productive conversation?

[WD: *Rather than me taking the lead concerning understanding her issue with procrastination, I begin by inviting Sarah to take the lead.*]

[Sarah: *That immediately indicated to me that I was going to be an active partner. And it encouraged me to focus and frame right away.*]

Sarah: OK. I think I've got a few areas of problems. One is I've got lots of ideas about what I want to write about and I struggle to focus on one idea, and within an idea I struggle to focus as well. And I think it's to do with my process, which is a second area. I don't seem to be able to do just a dirty draft of something and go back to it and refine it. I feel like I have that laborious process that you were talking about earlier[17] where I either look at every sentence and keep crafting and refining or I go off at a tangent because the issues that I'm looking at and wanting to write about have various connections and I end up, as I'm writing, connecting something else, and then I go off to that and have a look at that, but it has its own connections. So it's like an expanding mind map where I've got a central idea and then I go a away a way off and I find myself a way over here and think, 'How did I get here? How do I get back?' So there's a kind of processing.

Windy: Is this process prior to writing? Is this like a cognitive process that you engage in or is this after you've started to write?

Sarah: I think it's probably a bit of both. I do a lot of thinking in my head, and in my head it feels like it would be a real joy to write about because it's all in my head. I just need to get it down on paper. But it doesn't then translate into that. And then, as I'm doing it, I find myself, I'll have a central idea, then I'll have two or three points and then I'll go off on one of them and think, 'Right, what do I want to write about that?' And, as I'm doing that, my brain will be thinking, 'Oh yeah, but that links to that and to that and to that,' and it just constantly goes. I think I probably talk a bit like that as well; that I want to capture everything and explain everything.

Windy: Because in case what? If you don't, what?

Sarah: It's a wee bit like being at school. You know they used to say, 'Show your working?' It feels like I want to show my working for some reason, and it

---

[17] Sarah is referring to the presentation on 'Writing Procrastination' that I made during the first half of the workshop. This demonstration took place in the second half of the workshop.

might be to do with justifying what I think or how I got to where I think.

Windy: To whom?

Sarah: ... Well, that's the third area: I wonder if I have the right to write and I have linked to that the right to think what I think, and therefore the right to share what I want to share.

Windy: So, if we were to take one of those issues and really focus on it, not only for the purpose of our conversation, but maybe as a way of actually serving as a model for you, which one of those should we focus on and agree to stick to?

[Sarah: *I found the phrase 'and agree to stick to' interesting at the time and reading it now. It felt a very clear sort of contracting/expectation and responsibility-setting. A boundary I had to pay attention to.*]

[WD: *Sarah has mentioned three features of her writing procrastination, and here, I invite her to focus on one. Working towards an agreed focus is a typical feature of SST.*]

Sarah: ... So either the process or the right to write.... [*Long pause*] Maybe the right to write.

Windy: Right. By right to write, you mean R.I.G.H.T to W.R.I.T.E, do you?

Sarah: (*laughs*) Yes!

Windy: Could you just say a little bit about what you mean by 'right'?

[WD: *Once we have decided to focus on what Sarah calls her 'right to write', I clarify what she means by 'right' here. This is a typical feature of my work as an SST therapist where if I don't understand how a person is employing a term, I ask for clarification.*]

Sarah: ... Firstly, because I probably have some critical voices going around, one right back to childhood to my dad who told me one day, 'Who thinks anybody's interested in what you have to say?' and that's how life in the family was with him.

Windy: Do you agree with him?

[Sarah: *I found that interesting too – in the moment. You immediately gave me power to have my own opinion in a relationship where I rarely had that.*]

Sarah: No, I never did.

Windy: It may have been difficult to articulate it, but what was your response to that: 'Who's interested in what you've got to say?'?

Sarah: Indignation, frustration.

Windy: If we were to look at it in terms of the content – I understand you'd be angry about that, but, if we just have a look at the actual factual answer, who would be interested in what you've got to say?

Sarah: I guess then as a child, to be honest, I didn't really know.

Windy: How about now?

Sarah: But now I still feel ... I think I'm a wee bit like Marmite – people either get me or they really don't.

Windy: Fine. So you've got a 50% chance of people getting you. Is that a good enough number?

Sarah: I don't actually know if it's 50%.

Windy: OK, let's even say 25% of people get you and 75% don't. Is that a good enough number?

Sarah: When you put it like that … it is because it's 25 people.

Windy: Out of 100, yeah. So the answer to your question, which is do you have the right to write, would be what?

              [Sarah: *That felt a real 'keeping me on track' to answer your question. And your brevity facilitated mine.*]

Sarah: Yes, I do.

Windy: Right. And who can take that right away from you?

Sarah: The only person's me, I think.

Windy: Is there anybody else?

Sarah: … [*Pause*] I guess it depends if I write … under the auspices of someone else, then I have to meet their needs.

Windy: What do you mean by the auspices of someone else?

Sarah: Well, I did an article for a professional journal and it was turned down, but it was the way it was turned down – I didn't conform to some sort of way of putting something and they totally didn't get what I was trying to say, to the point where I went back to read it and thought, 'How could they have got that from it?'

Windy: But does that mean that you don't have a right to write or that means that they have a right not to publish what you write?

Sarah: I think it felt like I don't have the right to talk about this sort of stuff.

Windy: Because that's been determined by what?

Sarah: Because it was a professional body and I was writing about something to do with counselling and psychotherapy, and therefore, if that was their reaction, and it was, 'If you think this is worth writing about, then you've not been paying attention for the last 10 years,' or something, 'to CPD,' and I was like, 'My God, if that was true I should never have been a counsellor.'

Windy: But the point is, the fact that they turned your article down, does that deprive you of the right to write?

[Sarah: *I found this intervention a bit scary (keep on track) and also helpful (it cut to the chase).*]

Sarah: Only if I let it.

Windy: Right. So who's in charge of determining whether you have a right to write?

Sarah: Me.

Windy: I'm sorry, I'm getting a bit hard of hearing in my old age. What?

Sarah: (*laughs*) Me!

Windy: OK, you! By the way, that's called the Hard of Hearing Old Person's Technique.

[Sarah: *I thought that was brilliant at the time! It didn't just make me surer of what I wanted to say. It also made me vocalise a more assertive stance. It reinforced my power in a situation where I hadn't felt I had any.*]

Sarah: Well, it worked 'cos it made me surer of what I wanted to say.

Windy: OK. So we've established then that you have the right to write.

[WD: *In striving to understand Sarah's issue with the 'right to write,' the purpose of my questions was not only to clarify the issue but to help her to see that she, herself, is the person who can give and take away from her that right, irrespective of the views and responses of significant others.*]

Sarah: OK.

Windy: So the next time you start to think about, 'Do I have the right to write?' how are you going to respond?

Sarah: I'm going to remind myself that I do. I'm going to write something, near me that says, 'You have the right to write,' and giving myself the right to write.

[WD: *This is an example of a person rehearsing the solution in the session.*]

Windy: Right. And do you know what response to anybody who tells you, you don't have the right to write is?

Sarah: I have the right to write and I give myself that right.

Windy: I'm not suggesting you say that out loud, but you could actually say that in your head. So how are you gonna hang on to what we've talked about here in terms of, 'I've got the right to write,' so that you can take away and actually make use of it going forward?

[WD: *Here, I encourage Sarah to make an action plan where she can implement to solution.*]

Sarah: I'm going to write something that I have on the wall … to remind myself about that, because I think what was interesting, that percentage when you said, '50/50', and I thought, 'I don't think it is that', and you said, '25'. I was surprised at my reaction. It wasn't, 'Oh, that's nowhere near enough.' I really focused on who would be interested rather than who wouldn't, and I wonder how I can capture that and keep that.

Windy: Yeah, how can you keep that? Can you make a visual representation of 25 and 75?

[WD: *In response to her 'wondering' I suggest a visual representation of the point that Sarah wanted to keep hold of. Such visual representations can be powerful and memorable.*]

Sarah: Something about different sizes. I'd focus on this number of the 75, but actually, I don't know, I've got a sense of some little purple figure.

Windy: Do you like gardening?

[WD: *As Sarah was talking, I came up with an image of a watering can and did not register that she came up with her own image. However, she said later that she thought my example was 'brilliant'.*]

Sarah: I wouldn't say I like it.

Windy: I don't like gardening anyway, but for somebody who doesn't like gardening I come up with all of these gardening images. So what about a picture, you've got 75 and 25, holding a gardening can, watering the 25?

[WD: *I suggest this as a visual way of encouraging Sarah to keep her focus on those that might be interested in what she has to say rather than on those who might not be.*]

Sarah: … Like that.

Windy: Yeah?

Sarah: Yep.

Windy: What do you like about it?

Sarah: It's playful, which is bringing back some of the joy into all of this. For some reason I've got a sense of it being sunny. It needs water because it's sunny. I like the idea of growth. … [*Pause*] It's playful. I like the playfulness of it.

[WD: *Sarah has re-introduced the idea of joy into an activity that has become very serious and heavy for her*]

Windy: OK. So shall we go onto having a look at the other issue that you wanted to talk about?

[WD: *As we are about halfway through the session, I invite Sarah to select a second issue to discuss. This is always a bit of a dilemma for me as an SST therapist. Should I suggest that we end the session so that she can concentrate on one important takeaway, or should I help her with another linked issue and run the risk of compromising this takeaway? I decide to proceed, but ideally, I should raise this dilemma with the person and have her make the decision. I did not raise it because I did not experience it as a dilemma at the time.*]

Sarah: Yeah, thanks. My process.

Windy: Yeah. So tell me a little bit about what's problematic about your process in terms of writing, from your perspective?

Sarah: I seem to take ages to do not very much. I … [*long pause*] don't know if I've found the right environment and timing for things, because I think if I wrote I would actually really go at it for a long time, whereas I feel that I shouldn't keep writing for a long time. So there's the environment and maybe doing it in the way that suits me, that would mean doing it for longer, really spending a day on it or something and not having a break or whatever or not really having breaks.

Windy: Are you gonna be able to fit that into the way you live your life?

[WD: *As she speaks, Sarah outlines a possible practical solution to her second issue. In my experience, it is important that a person can integrate a solution into their life, otherwise they will not be able to maintain it. Hence my question here.*]

Sarah: I retired as a counsellor, yep. So I do have time. So I can do that.

Windy: Where would you do that?

[WD: *Having established that she can integrate that solution into her life, I ask Sarah to develop this by considering* where *she would implement the solution.*]

Sarah: Probably here.... I share a study with my husband. He tends to take it at certain times, but I could take it at different times.

Windy: And you can negotiate a time that would work?

Sarah: Yeah, and there's another space I could work in. We can split the space.

Windy: OK, so that's the environment bit. You say, 'Look, my sense is that I can see myself choosing to write for a long period of time in my study.' And, so the process that you spoke about before, the way it seemed to me, it's almost like you start off with something and then something comes to mind and then you follow it.

Sarah: Yes.

Windy: Is that your natural cognitive process?

Sarah: Yep. It really is like a mind map.

Windy: OK, that's fine. The thing about a mind map, some people use a mind map because they think like that and one thing goes to another and then they've got the map. A map is there to then point to a direction which you then can say, 'Wait a minute, I can start there and I've got that.' I mean books are linear. We haven't yet found a way of actually having a circular book. So they are linear, so you do need to then find a linear pattern from the mind map. Do you do that?

Sarah: ... I don't. I feel like the mind map's in my head. I don't put it down.

Windy: What would happen if you put it down?

[Sarah: *I found this helpful. It challenged me to think about the impact of doing something differently. A lot of your questions led me to think 'why don't I...?' And I found the answers put things into stark focus so quickly and easily solutions felt well within my grasp.*]

Sarah: I'm just thinking that would be much better. I mean, it seems so obvious in a way.... It seems so obvious in a way.... [*Pause*] Why wouldn't I do that? It's really weird. I'm just sitting here wondering why I don't do that. I'm not using a process that actually captures my internal processes.

[WD: *Through our discussion, we have discovered that Sarah is not using one of her strengths—'mind-map' thinking—to help her solve the problem, She could write her ideas down into a mind map.*]

Windy: That's right. One of the things about single-session therapy that we like to do is to really get people to identify and utilise their strengths, and it sounds like one of your strengths is that you do have a mind which can associate things and it ends up with a mind map, but it's a mind map that's a bit like the old idea or even a new idea of a map – you look at it. And you've got a mind map which you don't look at because it's in there[18] and it's not there.[19] I'm wondering what would happen if you did externalise it.

Sarah: It just feels like it would be so much easier because, as you're saying that, I'm realising how much energy I use to hold it in my head and not put it out there. And it's also making me think of when I was doing uni exams, we used to do four essays in three

---

[18] I am pointing to my head.
[19] I am pointing to a piece of paper.

hours, and I used to spend the first 20 minutes writing a five-minute plan for each essay. So, if I was running out of time or I'd forgotten what I thought, I had it there and I could refer to it. And it seems like why don't you extrapolate that out and do it here? Why don't you do the mind map?

Windy: Well, you can ask yourself the question why don't you or you could say, 'I'm going to do that.'

Sarah: Or you could do it.

Windy: Yeah.

Sarah: I am going to do it. Just crazy. Crazy I haven't done it before now.

Windy: Yeah, play to your strength.

Sarah: Yep.

Windy: Did you have some idea that somehow you shouldn't do that and somehow you should be able to write something without that?

[WD: *Here, I enquire whether there is an obstacle to Sarah implementing her own suggested solution.*]

[Sarah: *As before, this also made me think differently. I was going round in circles with 'what' I was doing or not doing. Your questions got me out of that unconscious cycle (however obvious it might seem!). Plus, if I name something, I can do something about it.*]

Sarah: … I think I was seeing it as a weakness, that I couldn't just do it in my head. I don't know why. But that list you gave of conditions you need to start, one of them seemed to be for me, 'It's in your head, you know it's all there, you should be able to do it from there.'

Windy: Yeah. Well, as opposed to what? What could you then take away from our discussion on this particular point instead?

[WD: *Having identified the obstacle, I ask Sarah about how she can respond to the obstacle.*]

[Sarah: *There's something about what you're doing with these questions that my process really responded to. And, again, your brevity encouraged mine.*]

Sarah: That there's no shame in using a tool that helps me visualise what is in my head, and it's a bit of a no-brainer to do that.

Windy: Right. So it'll be interesting to see what happens when you do that.

Sarah: Yep.

Windy: You mentioned three points. What was the other one?

[WD: *We still have time, so I enquire about the third issue. I mentioned earlier my dilemma about how much to cover in a session. I proceed knowing that I will be offering Sarah a copy of the recording after the session and the transcript of our session when it has been done.[20] I also think that we were on a roll and I wanted to have a sense of completion by covering all the issues Sarah mentioned.*]

---

[20] Whenever I do live demonstrations of therapy, I offer the volunteers a recording and a transcript of the session. I ask them to email me if they want me to do this. Most do, and Sarah did.

Sarah: The other one was just ideas and having various ideas for things. I'm full of ideas about things I would like to write about that I observed while I was working but didn't have time while I was working to step back and look at it more fully.

Windy: Can you remember some of those?

Sarah: Yes, stuff about being highly sensitive and about disenfranchised grief.

Windy: Where do those ideas exist?

Sarah: The HSP stuff I've done an information website for people about lots of things that I've thought of, but I've got an idea: I want to write a book for people who don't know they're highly sensitive and could just pick it up and, for £10 or whatever, could learn something that I've seen with client after client after client. And it happened with me when I realised I was highly sensitive – suddenly the world made sense.

Windy: Could you utilise what we spoke about before, that somehow you have a right to write that book?

[WD: *This is another typical SST intervention. Enquiring whether a person can use one of their strengths that were previously identified.*]

Sarah: I feel I have more of a right to write that book because I am an HSP, I've worked laterally, exclusively with HSPs, I've done a website, I know it makes a difference to people because of the feedback I've had. So there's something about that I feel like I've got a bit more right to do that. And I have an idea about something that is a bit different and I want to write something more humorous than dense. I've got loads of bits around my laptop and printed out, lots of bits of it, and I haven't gone back to it for a while and I really need to. Some stuff's already there.

Windy: So you mean you need to put it in one place?

Sarah: I do, absolutely.

Windy: Once you've got it out there, could you utilise the mind map to put it all in one place? Is that another thing that you could do in terms of mind maps?

[WD: *Here, I enquire whether Sarah can generalise her learning from one area to another – another commonly used intervention in SST.*]

Sarah: Yeah.

Windy: So, if you brought what we've talked about, 'Look, I have a right to write this book,' I wouldn't say you have more of a right but you're talking about it from a sense of experience.

Sarah: Yes.

Windy: And so that's important. And that you could actually bring to that project your right to write it. You could bring to that project the idea that you can use mind maps to collate some of the disparate information that you can bring together and you can put it in a mind map.

Sarah: Yep.

Windy: And what would happen do you think if you did those two things and you brought it to this particular project?

Sarah: I think I'd get a whole renewed kind of energy around it.... There's something I need to get out of the way first, another commitment that I have, I need to get that done, but I want to return to it and I want to return to it with some joy. I love writing and I want to find that again because I've just got into a sense of trudging and going round and round in circles with the same things and it's taken away the joy. I want to write it for other people but I want to write it and get it out of my head, and I think a mind map and a Post-It note with 'I have the right to write' and an image of leaning over the fence and watering, not just the people but also the ideas.

Windy: The ideas, that's right. You could use the same things, not only to grow your audience in terms of the people, but you could also use it to actually grow and develop your ideas.

[Sarah: *I remember that moment as it happened. The idea of watering not just the people but the ideas. I loved that! The way the session had gone, I felt enthused, empowered and instead of feeling doubt (e.g. about the idea in my journal article being so roundly rejected), I felt trust and excitement in my ideas. Quite a turnaround!!*]

Sarah: Yes.

Windy: So why don't you put these things together and let's see how you're gonna summarise these points and see how they fit together in your mind?

[WD: *Having helped Sarah to apply her previously identified solutions to this third issue, I sense that we are approaching the end of the session. Consequently, I ask her to summarise what we have covered in the session. In SST, we ask the person to summarise the session rather than summarise it for them. In this way, we remain person-focused, and the person remains active.*]

[Sarah: *And something about giving the person responsibility for it (the summary and the action). A powerful reminder of agency.*]

Sarah: OK. Well, the first thing I think is the right to write and I'll do a note, I'll do something to make it a nice-looking note that I like the look of and remind myself of the right to write. I will get a representation, a visual representation of the gardening image. And I will start using mind maps for things that I am writing that are bigger than blogs and I'll apply that to what I do and get back to what I did as a uni student, which was planning and setting out, and it's just that this mind map will be bigger than a five-minute plan for a single essay. And I'll colour-code it and stuff because I like colours. So I'm going to make it pleasant to look at.

[Sarah: *The colour was something I hadn't mentioned before, and it was an example of buy-in and enthusiasm for the possibilities.*]

Windy: When you were a uni student what strengths did you bring to the studying process then?

[WD: *I use this opportunity to invite Sarah to identify, reconnect with and use, in the present, strengths she had in the past.*]

Sarah: … Planning … [*pause*] curiosity … [*pause*] structure.

Windy: Planning, curiosity and structure. Do you still have those in the Sarah Army?

[WD: *I do like to use humour in my SST sessions. One of the ways I do this is to play around with words. 'Sarah army' refers to the 'Salvation army'.*]

[Sarah: *I absolutely loved the Sarah Army!! A play on words and my name. And a humorous way to remind me that I had a host of tools to use and that I wasn't on my own (which was a theme of my early life and always a joy to be reminded that I'm not now).*]

Sarah: I'm going to write that down as well and have some sort of image for that. I've certainly got curiosity. I think structure has become a bit of a barrier.... Instead of something that was helpful, I think it's become a barrier and it's stopped me; it's contributed to me.

Windy: How did you convert structure from a skill to a barrier?

Sarah: ... I think it's to do with volume. I think it was more manageable in the uni examples. It was one essay and I had a deadline so I had to get on with it. Whereas now I'm not sure I've finished my thinking on the subjects that I want to write about.

[WD: *From her summary and the subsequent exchange, we have identified another major block in Sarah's writing. She thinks she needs to finish her thinking about a subject before she writes about it. I address this below.*]

Windy: So when are you going to finish the thinking on that?

Sarah: ... [*Pause*] I can't honestly answer that.

Windy: I can.

Sarah: Right, OK. Help me out then.

Windy: When you're dead.

Sarah: Right. So it's that attainable, is it!?

Windy: Well, if I had that same philosophy, 'I haven't finished my thinking yet. I can't write until I finish my thinking,' I wouldn't have any books. Some people might think that would be a good idea, but, again, I think that's a condition you've got: 'I've got to finish my thinking first before I start writing.'

[WD: *I use self-disclosure here to indicate that if I had the same idea about finishing my thinking on a subject before writing about it, I would not have finished any books.*]

[Sarah: *I found the self-disclosure really helpful. If you – author of so many books – never finished your thinking, then it was nonsense for me to expect to!*]

Sarah: Yes, I really do.

[Sarah: *This whole section was a revelation. This thought – that I had to finish my thinking – had been at the edge of my thinking but never front and centre. Suddenly it was and it was, very helpfully, demolished.*]

Windy: How are you gonna rethink that idea?

Sarah: Your reaction has made me laugh at it, which is a good start 'cos it's taken the seriousness out of it. ... And, when you verbalise it and I say it and think about it, it does feel like, 'When are you ever gonna finish you're thinking?' And, actually, I think that's a key problem for me: I feel like I need to finish my thinking before I can do anything with it, and that's just a recipe for going round in circles. I think that's captured in a nutshell what's been going on.

Windy: Yeah, exactly. I remember years ago when I was a university lecturer and one of my students, I think they got together and thought they'd play a trick on me. So they asked me a question and said, 'What do you think of this statement?' and they read it out to me, and I said, 'That's a ridiculous statement. Who wrote it?' and they said, 'You did.' And I said, 'Well, I've changed my mind.' So, the point is, even if you finish your thinking, what does that mean? There's no space for you to change your mind?

Sarah: Yeah. Again, when you say that, when you verbalise that, it's just crazy. When do we ever finish our thinking about anything? We wouldn't learn anything, we wouldn't be open to change. Yeah.

[WD: *Sarah has made an important point. Verbalising one's ideas can give the person an opportunity to stand back and evaluate them rather than keeping them in one's head. In a way there is a parallel between this and Sarah putting on paper her ideas so that she can stand back and view them. This parallel did not occur to me at the time and even if it did, I doubt whether I would have verbalised it as it would have distracted us both from bringing the session to a good conclusion.*]

Windy: One of the things that comes across to me as we talk, if I can give you a suggestion, I think you have gotten a lot out of the process of verbalising these things, and I'm wondering if you have somebody, and I'm not talking about a therapist, but somebody, almost like having a peer dialogue with, somebody who will give you the space to verbalise some of this stuff, because I think, when you verbalise, you're able to stand back and look at it. I think part of it is that you haven't had an opportunity to verbalise these things and you haven't really had a chance to look at it. And we know that, when you keep things in your head, they tend to get a little bit stuck in there without the lubrication of conversation.

[WD: *Here I am suggesting that Sarah consider using an external resource to help her. This is another commonly used intervention in SST.*]

[Sarah: *I remember feeling seen when you said that. It felt like you'd observed my process and what I'd got out of the session. Very validating – my process has often annoyed people.*]

Sarah: Yeah, they really do. They just rampage around and don't go anywhere.

Windy: So you may want to think about that. So, very briefly, what are you going to take away from this, one or two points that are going to help you go forward on this?

[WD: *After the summary, I ask Sarah to nominate her takeaways.*]

Sarah: Well, I'm going to take lots from it, thank you.

Windy: Good.

Sarah: So finishing my thinking – I'm gonna let that go. It's good to have seen that and I can let that go and realise how it's shackled me. I'm going to realise the importance of me being able to verbalise what I'm thinking about writing. I've never talked about my writing to anybody. So I'm gonna find somebody to do that with. And the things that I mentioned before, the 'right to write' note, the mind map, using a mind map, just thinking how that suits me colour-wise, can colour-code, can just get ideas down, see them, see how they connect. The gardening image and something about Sarah Army, I don't know, it just made me laugh. But, honestly, it's just brought the joy back. This has just brought the joy back, just the way the conversation's gone. I feel more playful about it.

[Sarah: *Something about the session kept me more focused and concise than usual. I also sound a bit more articulate at this point! Another impact of the session, the discoveries, the humour, a sense of rapport.*]

Windy: You came in, when I first saw you, I thought, 'This is a heavy, serious problem that she's got here', but the way you look now, you look lighter.

Sarah: Yeah, I feel it.

Windy: Shall we get their comments in the group?

Sarah: Yeah, sure.

[WD: *A common way of ending an SST session is to see if the person has any questions to ask or any observations to make that they would later regret not asking or making. I did not do this because the session came to a natural end.*]

[Sarah: *It did come to a natural end ... and I might have commented on my surprise at how much we covered, the clarity of the problems and the solutions, my joy at discovering and reconnecting to so many positives. Thank you!*]

5

Skills in Single-Session Therapy

Introduction

Single-session therapy (SST)[21] can be defined as an intentional endeavour where the client and therapist agree to meet for a single session with the intent of helping the client address their chosen concern in that session with the understanding that more help is available if needed. It is based on research that shows that the modal number of sessions that clients have internationally is '1' and that 70–80% are happy with that session given their current circumstances (Talmon, 1990; Hoyt & Talmon, 2014). Thus, while many clients can be helped in one visit, others require additional help. SST is best delivered in a context where help is provided at the point of need rather than at the point of availability.

One of my concerns as a trainer of single-session

---

[21] This chapter originally appeared as the following four articles and is included in this form here with the kind permission of the publisher:

Dryden, W. (2020). Skills in single-session therapy. Part 1: Creating and maintaining a focus. *European Journal of Therapy Theory, Research and Practice*, 4(4), 1–4. http://www.europeantherapy.eu/volumes/ volume-4-2020/volume-4-article-4/.

Dryden, W. (2022). Skills in single-session therapy. Part 2: Ways of Beginning the Session. *European Journal of Therapy Theory, Research and Practice*, 6(3), 1–4. https://ejctrap.nationalwellbeingservice.com/volumes/volume-6-2022/ volume-6-article-3/.

Dryden, W. (2024). Skills in single-session therapy. Part 3: Ways of working with problems and solutions. *European Journal of Therapy Theory, Research and Practice*, 8(2), 1–6. https://ejctrap.nationalwellbeing service.com/ volumes/volume-8-2024/volume-8-article-2.

Dryden, W. (2024). Skills in Single-Session Therapy. Part 4: Ways of ending the session. *European Journal of Counselling Theory, Research and Practice*, 8(3), 1–4. https://ejctrap.nationalwellbeingservice.com/volumes/ volume-8-2024/volume-8-article-3.

practitioners is that therapists in training are not taught how to help many clients who attend one therapy session. To practise SST effectively, therapists need to acquire a range of skills. In this chapter, I will discuss the skills they need to begin the single session, help create a focus for the session, work with problems and solutions and bring the session to a suitably good end.

Beginning the Session

Getting the session off to a good start is important, and as I will discuss in this chapter, there are several ways of doing this.

Ensuring Informed Consent

Like other ways of working with clients, the ethical practice of single-session therapy is based on the client giving their informed consent to proceed. As the term makes clear, informed consent has two components. The client needs to be informed about the nature of SST and once this has been done, they need to give their consent to proceed. Even if the client has read about SST on an agency's website or an independent practitioner, the therapist still needs to clarify that the client understands its nature.

Therapist: Before we start, what do you understand about what we are going to do today?

Client: Well, I was told that we would have one therapy session and that is it.

Therapist: That is not the case. I will endeavour to help you today with whatever you wish to discuss with me, but more help is available for you in the future if you think you need it.

Client: So, I am not restricted to one session

Therapist: Not at all. You may not need more than one session, but you are not restricted to one session.

Client: That sounds better.

Therapist: So, would you like to proceed on that basis?

Client: Yes, I would.[22]

Beginning the Session if There Has Been Pre-Session Preparation

There is a small group of single-session therapists who hold that SST should be a single session of therapy with no preparation or follow-up. However, the majority believe that these are a part of SST. When clients are invited to prepare for the session by completing a pre-session questionnaire, this should be taken into account when beginning the session (see Dryden, 2023 and Chapter 1, pp. 32–3).

Therapist: Thank you for completing the pre-session questionnaire.

Client: You are welcome:

Therapist: Would you mind if I refer to the questionnaire, if necessary, in the session?

Client: Not at all.

Therapist: Thanks. What changes, if any, have you noticed between completing the questionnaire and today's session?

The therapist proceeds according to the client's response to this question. If the client has noticed any changes, the therapist would begin with this and help them understand what occasioned the change and how it could be capitalised upon. On the other hand, if the client has not noticed any changes, the therapist would ask a question from one of the following sections.

---

[22] Gaining a client's informed consent is one aspect of contracting. Other issues including agreeing confidentiality and other practical issues are done in SST but lie outside the scope of this chapter.

In these sections, I will assume that the client has not done any pre-session preparation.

Beginning the Session by Focusing on Its Purpose

Many therapy organisations seek to introduce SST to reduce their waiting lists. However, while SST services have this effect, their intent is, as has already been discussed, to provide help at the point of need and to see if therapists can help clients achieve their therapeutic goals in a single session, knowing that more help can be accessed if needed. Given that SST has a purpose, this is reflected in the following opening question.

Therapist: From your perspective, what is the purpose of our conversation today?

Asking this question enables the therapist to quickly discover whether the client has a realistic view of the purpose of SST. If not, the therapist can be clear about what the client can do and what they can't, helping the therapist orient the client to the therapeutic potency of SST.

Beginning the Session by Asking About the Client's Problem

As most clients seek SST for help with a problem, another common way of beginning SST is for the therapist to be problem-focused.[23] For example:

Therapist: What problem, concern or issue would you like to discuss with me? or

Therapist: What problem, concern or issue would you like me to help you with?

Beginning the Session by Asking about the Client's Goals

In my view, when a person seeks help with a problem, they have a goal in mind – although they may need assistance to express

---

[23] A therapist who practises SST from a solution-focused perspective might decide *not* to ask a problem-focused question as they would want to be solution-focused in their questioning.

this – and the therapist needs to help the client identify a solution that effectively addresses the problem and helps them achieve their goal. I will discuss the skills that SST practitioners can use to help clients identify such solutions later in the chapter.

The goal-directed nature of SST is reflected in the following beginning questions.

Therapist: What would you like to achieve by talking with me today?

Therapist: What would you like to take away from our conversation that would make it worthwhile for you to come today?

In SST, I distinguish between a goal related to the client's nominated problem and a goal related to what the client wants to achieve by the end of the session. If the client mentions the former, the therapist can usefully ask about the latter and help the client see that the achievement of their session goal can serve as a prelude to the achievement of their problem-related goal.

Beginning the Session by Asking about What Help the Client Is Seeking

While most clients seem to want help solving an emotional problem in SST, other forms of help are available, and a different way of beginning a single session is to ask about the type of help the client is seeking from the therapist.

Therapist: How can I be most helpful to you today?

Therapist: What help would you like from me today?

If the client initially struggles to answer the question, the therapist should give them alternatives, as shown below.

Therapist: What help would you like from me today?

Client: I am not sure.

Therapist: Well, there are several ways in which I could be helpful. Would you like me to summarise them, and you can tell me which resonates most with what you think would be most helpful?

Client: That would be useful.

Therapist: Well. I could help you to develop a greater understanding of an issue; I could listen while you talk about an issue; I could help you to express your feelings about an issue; I could help you to solve an emotional or behavioural problem with which you feel stuck; I could help you to make a decision if that were relevant or I could help you resolve a dilemma. Do any of these describe the kind of help you are looking for?

Sometimes, a client may ask for help that the therapist is reluctant to give. In this case, it is important that the therapist is transparent about what they are prepared to do and what they are not prepared to do, as in the following.

Therapist: How can I be most helpful to you today?

Client: I would like you to advise me on which job offer to take.

Therapist: Well, therapy is very different from giving advice. So, I will not do that. However, I would be more than happy to look at the options that you have with you and help you figure out which course of action to take based on what is important to you rather than on what I think you should do. How does that sound?

Client: That sounds OK.

Beginning the Session: The Gloria Films

Perhaps the most famous films in psychotherapy's history have become known as the 'Gloria Films'.[24] In these films, 'Gloria' (not her real name) had what can be seen now as a single, 'one-off' session of therapy with each of three well-known therapists: Carl Rogers (the developer of what is now known as Person Centred Therapy), Fritz Perls (the developer of Gestalt Therapy) and Albert Ellis (the developer of what is now known as Rational Emotive Behaviour Therapy or REBT). Each session lasted 30 minutes or less. For the present purposes, I will consider and reflect on how each therapist began their session with 'Gloria'. As will be seen, each opening gambit reflects, to some degree, the central ideas of the approach to therapy being demonstrated. This shows that the therapist's assumptions underpin even simple beginning questions.

Carl Rogers: Now then, we have half an hour together, and I do not know what we will be able to make of it, but I hope we can make something of it. I would be glad to know whatever concerns you.

Here, Rogers's beginning statement to Gloria is tentative, hopeful, and invitational, reflecting the person-centred approach. However, the phrase 'whatever concerns you' directs Gloria to her concerns and is thus somewhat inconsistent with the approach. A less directive phrase here would have been, 'I would be happy to know whatever you choose to tell me.'

Fritz Perls: We are going to have an interview for half an hour.

Here, Perls is mercurial, descriptive and in the here and now in how he begins the session. This is consistent with Gestalt Therapy principles and Perls' practice of them.

Albert Ellis: Well, would you like to tell me what's bothering you most?

---

[24] The formal title of these films was 'Three Approaches to Psychotherapy'. They were produced in 1965 by Everett Shostrom (1965).

Here, Ellis is consistent with the problem-focused nature of REBT, although inconsistent with the *ABC* model propounded by the approach.[25] His statement implies a causality (something at *A* bothers the client at *C*), which is at variance with the model. A more accurate beginning would have been, 'Well, would you like to tell me what you are bothered about most?' Here, *C* is deemed to be about *A* and not caused by it.

Conclusion

How a single-session therapist begins the session in SST has a decided influence on the way the session is likely to unfold. Here, I have discussed different foci the therapist may utilise and provided some key questions associated with each focus. I then looked at how three well-known therapists initiated a single session with the same client and discussed how consistent their opening was with the theory underpinning each approach.

Creating and Maintaining a Focus

In this section of the chapter, I will discuss the skills involved in working with the client to create a focus for the session and how to maintain this focus once it has been created.

Helping the Client to Create a Focus for the Session

Once the client has informed consent to participate in single-session therapy, the therapist's primary goal is to help the client create a focus for the session. When one has been created the therapist needs to help the client to maintain this focus.

The single-session therapist can help the client create a focus by asking several questions. These questions can be problem-oriented, solution-focused, or goal-focused. In SST, a solution helps the person address their problem effectively to achieve their goal.

---

[25] Here, *A* stands for adversity, *B* stands for the person's basic attitude towards the adversity and *C* stands for the emotional, behavioural and thinking consequences of the basic attitude.

Questions that help create a problem focus for the session

- What is your most pressing concern that I can help you address today?
- What one issue can I help you with today?

Questions that help create a solution focus for the session

- If I could help you today to address your problem effectively, what would your response be?
- If I could help you find a solution to your problem today that you could take forward to achieve your goal, would you be interested?

Questions that help create a goal focus for the session

- What would you realistically like to have achieved by the end of the session which would make you glad that you came today?
- If when you are at home this evening, and you reflect on our session today what would you have realistically liked to have achieved?

After the therapist has asked the client a focus-oriented question, the client's response will either indicate that a focus can be created from that response or that the therapist needs to ask further clarificatory questions. It is also important to note that the therapist may begin by asking for a problem focus and then, depending on the client's response, use that to agree on a solution or a goal focus. This also occurs in the following exchange.

Therapist: What one issue can I help you with today?

Client: I have been quite anxious lately.

Therapist: Anxious about what?

Client: I am anxious about my son not getting into the school of his choice.

Therapist: What effect does your anxiety have on you?

Client: I have sleepless nights and cannot concentrate on my work.

Therapist: How do you hope I can help you with this problem today?

Client: Help me get some sleep and concentrate on my work.

Therapist: So, if I can help you address your anxiety about your son's schooling so that you can sleep and concentrate on your work, what would you think of that?

Client: That would be great.

Therapist: So, shall we agree that this will be the focus of the session

Client: Yes.

Helping the Client to Maintain the Agreed Focus

Once the therapist and client have agreed on a focus, both must maintain this focus if they are going to use session time well. It is the therapist's primary task to ensure that this focus is maintained. The therapist uses a variety of skills to do this.

Seeking and Gaining Permission to Interrupt the Client

When I received training as a therapist 50 years ago, interrupting the client was strictly forbidden. The therapist's primary task was to encourage the client to explore their concerns and to follow them in their exploration rather than to guide it in any direction. Therefore, there was no reason to interrupt the client. Apart from that, interrupting the client was seen as rude. In single-session therapy, interrupting is regarded very differently. Once a session focus has been agreed upon, the therapist needs to take charge to maintain it during the session. As interrupting the client *may* be seen by the latter as being rude, the therapist first provides a rationale for doing so and then seeks permission from the client. Here is an example:

Therapist: We have now agreed on a focus for the session; we both need to maintain this focus. OK?

Client: OK.

Therapist: In any conversation between two people, it is easy for one or both to go from topic to topic and in a social conversation, that is perfectly fine, but in a therapeutic conversation, when we have agreed on a focus, that is problematic. So, if that happens with us, I would like to interrupt you to bring us back to the focus. I will strive to do that as sensitively as possible, but I will need to do this. Do I have your permission to do so?

Client: Yes, that is fine. I do tend to meander around sometimes.

Therapist: Feel free to interrupt me if I go off topic too.

Client: (*laughing*) I will.

Checking that Both Are Maintaining the Focus

Sometimes, it is difficult for the therapist to know whether or not a client has wandered away from an agreed-upon focus. Thus, what appears, at first sight, to be a departure from the focus may be a vital elaboration on a topic that clarifies the focus. Mutual dialogue is a critical feature in SST, so when this happens, the therapist checks with the client to ensure that the focus is being maintained.

Therapist: Can I just check something with you?

Client: OK.

Therapist: We agreed to focus on your anxiety about your son's schooling, and I am aware that we are now discussing your wife spending much time with her sister. I am not sure how this fits with your anxiety about your son's schooling.

Client: It does not. I was going off track.

Therapist: So, shall we get back to your feelings of anxiety about your son not getting into his preferred school?

Client: Yes.

In the exchange above, the client acknowledges that they had gone off track. The following is an example where what seems to be a departure from the focus clarifies the focus.

Therapist: Can I just something check with you?

Client: OK.

Therapist: We agreed to focus on your anxiety about your son's schooling, and I am aware that we are now discussing your daughter's problems at ballet school. I am not sure how that fits with your anxiety about your son's schooling.

Client: The way I see it, they are both instances of my anxiety that my children may be blocked from getting what they want in life.

Therapist: OK, I get that. They are linked. Would it make sense for us to maintain the focus on your son and then see if we can generalise to the situation with your daughter?

Client: If we could do both today, that would be great.

Therapist: OK, let us do that.

In this latter exchange, the client's seeming departure from the agreed focus (anxiety about the client's son's schooling) clarified the focus (anxiety about the client's children not getting what they want in life). The former is a specific example of the latter, and the client's introduction of his daughter was another example of the broader focus. Note how the therapist acknowledged the link and suggested they remain with the specific instance of the now broadened focus (anxiety about the client's son's schooling). The therapist then indicated that the client could generalise any learning to the other particular instance of the broadened focus (anxiety about the client's daughter's difficulties at ballet school).

This latter example shows how the single-session therapist works with both the specific and the general in SST, ensuring that both types of issues are connected.

Conclusion

Using time effectively in single-session therapy is a core skill in this form of service delivery. Here, I have discussed the important skills of helping clients create and maintain an agreed-upon focus so that they can get the most from their time with the therapist.

Ways of Working with Problems and Solutions

Most clients come to single-session therapy seeking a solution to an emotional and/or behavioural problem with which they are stuck (Dryden, 2025). In doing this solution-focused work, the single-session therapist needs to be able to work skilfully with problems and solutions. In this paper, I will outline and discuss such work.

Working with Problems[26]

In single-session therapy, we tend to work with the problem or issue selected by the client. I call this the 'nominated' problem. However, how we ask for such a problem influences the one that the client nominates.

---

[26] Therapists who practise solution-focused brief therapy and bring this to their single-session work may not work with problems.

Be careful what you ask for. Consider the following two questions:

- Question 1: 'What is the most important problem you want me to help you with?'

- Question 2: 'If I could help you with the problem that causes you the most significant concern today, which one would that be?

These two questions orient the client to their 'most important problem' or 'the problem that causes them the greatest concern'. However, what if the client does not want to discuss such a problem but wants help with a less important issue with which they are currently concerned? My view is that they may well choose to accede to the therapist's request and not discuss what they want to discuss.

Now consider this question:

- Question 3: 'Which problem would you like me to help you with today?'

My view is that this question affords the client the opportunity to discuss a problem of their choosing, whether this is an issue that causes them the greatest concern or not. Consider Martha, who has social anxiety, which she deems to be the problem that causes her the most concern. She comes to see a therapist because she wants help with procrastination over a term paper. My view is she is more likely to nominate her problem with procrastination when she is asked the third question than when she is asked the first two questions.

Agreeing the nominated problem. Despite being asked for one problem they want to discuss in the session, a client may come up with two or more problems. If this happens, the therapist must explain to the client that they can be most helpful to the client by helping them with one problem but that in doing so, it *may* be possible to help the client to generalise any solution arrived at in response to their nominated problem to the client's other problem(s).

Understanding the nominated problem from the client's perspective. As with other modes of therapy delivery, it is important for the therapist to understand the client's nominated problem as the client sees it. Such empathic communication serves several purposes in SST. First, it serves to strengthen the bond between client and therapist. Second, it helps the therapist to understand the client's view of the problem, which may explain how the client unwittingly maintains it. Thus, if a client says that other people's stupidity causes their anger, this view shows that the person takes no responsibility for their feelings, which may serve to maintain their problem. The only way they think they can deal with their problem is to avoid what they consider to be other people's stupidity. The therapist will use this information later when helping the client to see how they unwittingly maintain their problem.

Assessing the problem. When assessing the client's nominated problem in SST, it is useful to ask for a specific example of this problem. This example may have occurred recently, which typically happens or stands out in the client's memory. I personally like to work with an anticipated (or future) example of the problem so that the client can apply a co-created solution to the same situation as we have been assessing. When working with a specific example of the client's nominated problem, it is useful to ask the client to describe: (i) where the example took place, (ii) who was present and (iii) what those present were doing.

It is here that the therapist will bring to the problem-based assessment concepts derived from their preferred orientations, if necessary. The therapist and client may employ such concepts later when they come to work to identify potential solutions to the client's problem.

Helping the Client to Understand How They Unwittingly Maintain the Problem One important part of the problem assessment is for the therapist and client to understand how the client has unwittingly maintained the problem. The main purpose of such strategies is to help the person to avoid immediate distress. While the therapist will look for idiosyncratic problem-maintaining factors, they will also keep in mind common problem-maintaining factors such as:

- Avoidance factors;
- Safety-seeking behaviour while remaining in the problem situation;
- Lack of social support;
- Meta-emotional problems (having an emotional problem about one's nominated problem;
- Compensatory behaviours;
- Negative thinking;
- Distress intolerance;
- Discomfort intolerance;
- Substance misuse. (Dryden, 2023)

Helping the client to set a problem-related goal and a session goal. The main purpose of problem assessment in SST is to help the client and the therapist understand what the client wants to achieve from discussing the nominated problem. I have already briefly discussed the issue of goal setting in SST in the previous two sections of this chapter. Here, I want to distinguish between a problem-related goal and a session goal.

PROBLEM-RELATED GOAL. A goal related to the client's problem is best identified when the problem has been assessed. Ideally, it needs to be specific, meaningful and provide a realistic and healthy emotional and behavioural response to the adversity at the heart of the problem. It is important for the therapist and client to acknowledge that the problem-related goal serves as a signpost for the client to work towards after the session, equipped with a solution co-created in the session.

SESSION GOAL. A session goal relates to what the therapist will help the client to achieve by the end of the session. Quite often, it represents a solution that, if implemented after the session, will help the client move towards achieving their problem-related goal.

Working with Solutions

As mentioned above, a solution in single-session therapy represents something that, if implemented by the client, will help them to effectively address their nominated problem and make progress towards their problem-related goal. There are several issues that need to be considered by both the therapist and the client in co-creating a solution.

The client is prepared to implement the solution. Whatever the solution the therapist and client decide upon, the client must be prepared to implement this solution. Otherwise, it will be theoretically viable but not practically so. It is important, therefore, for the therapist to help the client be mindful that they can integrate a potential solution into their life. Thus, for example, if the client and therapist decide that it is important for the client to exercise regularly, they will only do so if they can incorporate this into their daily schedule. Otherwise, no matter how good the solution is, it will not help the client if they do not act on it.

The solution is negotiated. Unless the client has the sense that they have fully contributed to the construction of the solution, then they may not be wholeheartedly committed to it. Consequently, the solution must be negotiated by the therapist and the client rather than given by the former to the latter.

Types of solutions. As single-session therapy is client-led, the therapist will help the client select whichever solution the client thinks is best for them, not which solution the therapist thinks is best for them. Various solutions may be negotiated between therapists and clients in single-session therapy. I have categorised them as follows.

REFRAMING SOLUTION. A reframe-based solution helps the person put a troublesome event into a new frame with the result that the problem is rendered non-problematic and can even be seen positively.

ATTITUDE CHANGE SOLUTION. An attitude is an evaluative stance that a person takes towards adversity. When a person has a problem with adversity, this is likely because they hold a rigid and extreme attitude towards it. The solution is helping the person develop an alternative flexible and non-extreme attitude towards the same adversity.

INFERENCE CHANGE SOLUTION. An inference is a person's hunch about reality, which may be correct or incorrect. Quite often, the client can never be sure about the validity of an inference and, therefore, can be encouraged to accept the 'best bet' about what happened, is happening or will happen.

SOLUTION BASED ON A CHANGE IN THE PERSON'S RELATIONSHIP WITH THE PROBLEM. This solution is effected by the therapist facilitating a shift in the client's relationship with their problem. This may involve them recognising that what they saw as a dysfunctional response to adversity is, in fact, quite an understandable one which many people would have made. This helps the person accept their response's existence rather than fight against it.

BEHAVIOURAL CHANGE SOLUTION. A solution based on a behaviour change involves the person taking action or refraining from taking action. In the former, the hope is that when the client changes their behaviour, they invite a different response from another person with whom they have a problem. In the latter, the client refrains from taking action rather than acting in self-defeating ways (e.g., in substance misuse issues).

SITUATIONAL CHANGE SOLUTION. Sometimes, a person is best served if they change a situation that they are in. For example, a person may be working for a hyper-critical boss, and if no other solution will help the person, it is probably in their best interest to get a new job.

CHANGE BASED ON A COMBINATION OF SOLUTIONS. While sometimes a person needs a single solution to their problem (e.g., reframing), they may also need a combination of solutions. For example, if a person needs to assert themselves with someone, they need to change not only their behaviour but also their attitude in a way that supports the assertion.

Potential solution sources. Often, a solution to the client's nominated problem emerges from the therapist and client's conversation about the latter's nominated problem. As this conversation unfolds, the therapist keeps in mind several potential sources for the solution.

OPPOSITE TO MAINTAINING FACTORS. As discussed above, a client may implement several strategies that deal with their initial distress but serve to maintain the problem. Understanding these maintenance factors is useful in that their opposite can serve as part of the solution to the problem. The most obvious of these are as follows:

HELPFUL FEATURES FROM PREVIOUS ATTEMPTS TO SOLVE THE NOMINATED PROBLEM. The client has likely tried to help themself or seek help for the problem before. While such help will not have proven completely effective – otherwise, the person would not be seeking help now – it is quite possible that some of these help-seeking attempts will have proven helpful to the client. Consequently, it is useful for the therapist to help the client to identify such strategies as they can for the basis of the solution that the client is seeking.

WHAT HAS HELPED WHEN THE CLIENT HAS SOLVED BOTH RELATED AND UNRELATED PROBLEMS BEFORE. It is also very likely that the client has solved emotional problems before in areas that are related to the nominated problem and not related to it. If so, the therapist can help the client identify these productive strategies and investigate if the client can employ them to solve their nominated problem.

THE CLIENT'S STRENGTHS. While the client is seeking help because they feel unable to deal with the nominated problem by themself, they likely have personal strengths that are manifest in other areas of their life that they do not recognise or if they do recognise them, they do not think that they can apply these strengths to the solution of the nominated issue. The single-session therapist's task is to help them identify such strengths and see their applicability to the solution of their problem.

Strengths may be asked for directly (e.g., 'What strengths do you have as a person?') or can be inferred from what the client has been saying (e.g., 'You know, as I listen to you talk about what you have suffered, I am struck by how resilient you are. I wonder if when you stand back, you can recognise such resilience in yourself?').

Once a client recognises their strengths, the therapist can ask about their applicability to the solution of the nominated problem (e.g., 'How do you think you could apply this strength to the problem you have chosen to discuss with me?')

The applicability of identified and owned strengths can be investigated and harnessed to what the client and therapist have decided might be the best solution to the client's nominated problem.

THE EXTERNAL RESOURCES THAT ARE AVAILABLE TO THE CLIENT. External resources may include people, organisations, or help-related materials. The client may call upon one or more people whom they know and trust to provide different forms of help to the person. For example, one person may support the client as they implement their chosen solution, while another person may provide more specific help-related guidance.

External organisations may provide the client with different forms of help. One particular useful role that an organisation might play is to put the client in touch with people who have grappled and dealt effectively with similar problems so that the client can see how others have dealt with their nominated problem.

Help-related materials include self-help books, booklets and pamphlets and online and digital services that can provide both interactive and non-interactive assistance to the client

THE CLIENT'S ROLE MODELS. It is useful for the therapist to ask the client for a person who they look up to who may serve as a role model for dealing effectively with the problem. In helping the client to identify a role model, the person needs to be someone that the client thinks they can emulate, and that this person can offer a viable solution to the client's problem. The more the therapist helps the client to specify this solution, the better. It is important, of course, that the client can see themself implementing the solution and integrating this into their life.

THE CLIENT'S VIEWS ON POTENTIAL SOLUTIONS. The client may have a view of what is likely to be helpful to them, and the therapist is advised to elicit this information. The therapist needs to tread warily here. On the one hand, the client's view on this issue is to be respected; on the other hand, the therapist needs to adopt a professional stance towards the client's suggestion. If the therapist has any concerns about the client's views, then it is important that these need to be shared openly and with clarity. In the final analysis, the client is free to accept or reject the therapist's opinion.

THE THERAPIST'S VIEWS ON POTENTIAL SOLUTIONS. The final source for selecting an effective solution to the client's nominated problem comes from the therapist themself. In my view, given the emphasis in SST on client empowerment, it is best if the solution that is arrived at is based heavily on client variables. However, sometimes, the client needs more input from the therapist, and when this happens, I suggest that the client say something like, 'Would you be interested in my take on what might be helpful in solving your problem? It's not the only approach it is possible to take, but it is one that I think may be helpful to you.' The client is unlikely to say 'no' to this question, but how they say 'yes' reveals their attitude.

After the therapist offers their stance on the issue, the two can decide whether to take the therapist's suggestions forward and, if so, how.

The solution needs to be generalisable. A good solution is one that the client can generalise from their nominated to other related problems that they may have and to problems that might be unrelated to the nominated problem. However, if a solution works for the client's nominated problem but cannot be generalised, then the client should be encouraged to select it since they have only come for help for the nominated problem.

The solution needs to be rehearsed in the session if practicable.
Most solutions that the client and therapist co-create will need to
be rehearsed in the session to help the client discover if they can
see themself implementing the solution in everyday life. The
exception to this is where the solution is based on a reframe,
which, in general, when accepted by the client, requires no
rehearsal.

The client and therapist work together to find a way of
rehearing the solution in the session. This may best be done by
using imagery, behavioural rehearsal or role-play. Two-chair
dialogues have been used in SST to good effect in this respect
(Pugh, 2021). The rehearsal will lead to the client deciding that (i)
the solution is workable in its present form, needs no modification,
and they can see themself implementing it; (ii) the solution is
workable but needs tweaking to a greater and lesser degree after
which it is rehearsed in its modified form and the client commits
themself to implementing it or (iii) the solution is not viable in
which case the search for a viable solution is resumed.

Helping the client to implement the solution. Once the client has
selected a solution to which they can commit and which they
think has the potential to help them address their nominated
problem effectively, the therapist's task is to help them construct
an action plan to help them implement the solution in their
everyday life. It is important that the therapist helps the client see
in this respect that the effective implementation of the solution
depends on the client developing new habits of thought and/or
behaviour.

When developing an action plan, it is important for the
therapist to remember that they may not see the person again.
Thus, they are advised not to negotiate a specific task with the
client. Rather, they need to develop an action plan where:

- The purpose of the solution is firmly in the client's mind.
- The solution to be implemented is very clear.

- The times when the solution is to be implemented are agreed.
- The frequency with which the solution is to be implemented is also agreed.
- If the solution is to be implemented with other people, these people should be specified in the plan.
- Any potential obstacles to solution implementation are identified and a plan is devised to deal with them.

It is important for both therapist and client to keep at the forefront of their minds the fact that the more the client can integrate the action plan into their everyday life, the more likely it is that they will be able to implement it.

In the final part of this chapter on the skills needed to practise single-session therapy effectively, I will discuss how best to end a single session.

Ways of Ending the Session

The skills needed to bring the session to a satisfactory conclusion concern: (i) encouraging the client to summarise the session; (ii) ensuring that the client is clear about what they are going to take away from the session; (iii) giving the client an opportunity to generalise their learning, if relevant; (iv) reviewing the possibilities for the future and (v) taking time to answer any last-minute questions that the client may have and giving them space to say anything that want to say that they have not said. The main goal of ending the session is to have the client leave the session with their morale restored, hopeful that what they have discussed will make a difference to their life going forwards.

How to Judge When the Session Is Approaching an End

I am often asked about the length of a single session of therapy (Dryden, 2022b). There is no set answer to this question, but it can range from 20 mins to three hours. Thus, one way of determining when the session is coming to an end is by the clock. However, in my view this is not the most effective way of making this judgment. A better way is to consider what issues have been covered and when the therapist has helped the client to make an action plan to implement their chosen solution to their nominated problem is a good sign that the session is entering its end phase (Dryden, 2024b). When this sign occurs, the therapist should initiate the end of the session first by inviting the client to summarise the session.

Encouraging the Client to Summarise the Session

Summarising is a key therapeutic skill that those on initial therapy training courses learn as part of their basic therapy skills module. The purpose of summarising is to synthesise a large amount of data for the client so that the work can stay focused. The therapist's use of summarising can occur at the beginning of a session (to review what was covered in the previous session), during the session (to help maintain the focus of that session) or at the end of the session (to review what was covered in the session).

In single-session therapy, summarising is used mainly at the end of the session but with one major difference. The therapist asks the client to summarise the session rather than summarise the session for the client. The reason for this is twofold. First, it invites the client to be actively engaged in the session throughout, an important principle in SST. By contrast, a therapist-provided summary renders the client passive. Second, in making the summary, the client is trusted to articulate what they deem to be important in the session. In a therapist-provided summary, the therapist articulates their view on what was important.

Clients are sometimes taken aback when asked to provide a summary of the session. For example:

Therapist: We are coming to the end of the session. Perhaps you would like to summarise what we covered.

Client: I'm not very good at things like that. Can you summarise it for me?

Therapist: I could but I would only be covering what seemed important to me. I am much more interested to find out what seemed important to you.

Client: OK. That makes sense.

Once the client has provided their summary, the therapist may suggest one or two additions that the client may have forgotten. However, the client should be encouraged to add those points only if they are deemed important by the client themself, not because the therapist suggested them.

A good client summary ideally includes:

- The client's nominated issue;
- A review of the work the therapist and client did on the issue;
- The solution that the client developed and rehearsed, if relevant;[27]
- The action plan that was developed, if relevant;[28]
- Any other takeaways the client deems important.

Clarifying Client Takeaways

In single-session therapy, a client takeaway is a point deemed significant by the client that if acted upon has the potential to promote constructive cognitive, affective and behavioural change.

Note that in their summary the client may: (a) mention their selected solution as the main or only takeaway, (b) mention their solution and one or more takeaways, (c) mention other takeaways but not the solution. If the latter happens then the therapist should enquire about the omission of the solution. The client may have forgotten it or it may indicate that they are not invested in the solution. In which case, the therapist should focus on their other takeaways as a guide for future action.

It is good practice to suggest that the client make a note of both their solution and other relevant takeaways for later reference. This also applies to their action plan.

When holding a single-session therapy mindset, the therapist

---

[27] While most single-session work is solution-focused, this is not universally the case (Dryden, 2025). Thus, the client's summary may not include a solution and an action plan.
[28] See footnote 27.

remembers that in the session 'less is more' and 'more is less'. Consequently, the more takeaways the client lists in addition to their selected solution, the less they are likely to take away from the session. As such, it is useful to encourage them to prioritise among their takeaways. In this case, it is useful to ask the client a question such as:

Therapist: Setting aside the solution, which of the takeaways you mentioned is it most helpful for you to remember and act on?

Determining if the Client Can Generalise Their Learning

One of the criticisms that conventional therapists make of SST is that while it may help the client with their nominated issue, it does little else. Setting aside the view that often clients have only come to SST for help with a single issue and are happy if they have been helped with this, there is more that the single-session therapist can do, if the client is interested. First, the client can have more help later if they want to. But even if they only choose to attend for one session, the therapist can raise with them the possibility of generalising their learning from the example of their nominated issue to other relevant examples of the issue and also from their nominated issue to other issues that they may have. In my experience most clients don't think of generalising their therapeutic learning unless the therapist raises this as something that they may benefit from doing.

Here are some examples of a therapist encouraging the client to generalise their learning:

Therapist: Can you think of other examples of your fear of speaking in public where you can apply what you learned about dealing with this issue at your next seminar?

Therapist: Are there other problems that you have where you can apply what you have learned about effectively addressing your public-speaking fear?

Reviewing Future Possibilities

An integral part of single-session therapy is that the client needs to implement what they have learned from the session before deciding to seek further help. It is important therefore for the therapist to explain to the client that they will not be able to make another appointment at the end of the session because they have not yet had the opportunity to get as much from the current session.[29] There are two possibilities:

- The client is encouraged to reflect on what they have learned from the session, digest this learning, act on it, let time pass and then decide if they need further help. Normally, the client will be told from which date they are allowed to access such help if they choose to do so and they can do this.

- The agency in which the client is being seen informs the client that they will be contacted after the session (usually 2–3 weeks after) to see how the client is doing and if they need further help. Here the client is also encouraged to engage in the reflect-digest-act-wait-decide process.

In both cases, the therapist will outline the possibilities open to the client. These possibilities will vary according to which options are offered by the therapist or agency. The main point when outlining these options is that the therapist needs to state explicitly that each option is equally fine and that the client should select the one that suits them when the time comes. It is also important for the therapist to be clear with the client what the waiting times are for each of the available therapy options. Here is an example of this.

Therapist:　　When you come to decide on taking things forward, here are your options. Let me stress that each option is perfectly fine and the main point is that you select the one that is right for you. OK?

---

[29] An exception here would be if the client was highly disturbed at the prospect of not booking another session at the end of the current one.

Client: OK.

Therapist: When the time comes, you might decide that you have got what you wanted from this session and don't need further help. If you do decide to seek further help, the options are: (i) another session with me or another trained therapist. You can have this session a week after you contact us; (ii) a block of six therapy sessions with a trained therapist. I don't offer this service, Currently, there is a two-month wait for this service or (iii) ongoing therapy with one of our trainee therapists on placement with us. Currently, there is a three-month wait for this service. As I said, from our point of view, each option is perfectly fine.

Client: If I decide that I need further help, what would you recommend?

Therapist: The option that I outlined that you will think will be most helpful to you, bearing in mind the time you will have to wait for it.

Dealing with Any Last-Minute Issues

One of the major goals of SST is to help restore the morale of the client so that they leave the session with a degree of hope for the future (Frank, 1961). As such, we don't want the client to go away thinking later that they wished they had mentioned something to their therapist or asked them something since, if this was the case, it might distract them from the hope they derived from the session. As such, before the session ends, it is useful for the therapist to say something like:

Therapist: Is there anything you want to ask me about *the issue we have been discussing* that later you would regret not asking me, or is there anything you wish to tell me about *the issue we have been discussing* that later you would regret not telling me?

It is vital that the client does not use this as an opportunity to begin to tell the therapist about a second issue that they have. This is why I have italicised 'the issue we have been discussing', and I recommend that therapists stress this when asking their clients this question.

In this chapter, I have detailed some of the skills needed to practise single-session therapy effectively from beginning to end. I hope I have succeeded in this end.

6

Sign Up, Meet Up, Speak Out: Single Sessions in the Context of Meetup Groups

Overview

From 2012 to 2020, I ran an in-person meetup group in London from a CBT perspective.[30] A typical group lasted two hours and included me giving a lecture on a psychological theme and two single sessions where I worked with people from the audience (predominantly professional, but with some non-professionals in attendance) who sought help for problems related to the lecture's theme. In this chapter, I present data on the themes raised by volunteers and outline how I tend to work in these sessions. The meetup group ended in 2012 due to COVID-19 restrictions.

The Context

The single-session work that I discuss in this chapter took place in the context of a meetup group known as the 'UK CBT' meetup group. Meetup is a service used to organize online groups that host in-person events for people with similar interests. The UK CBT meetup group is for people interested in Cognitive

---

[30] An earlier version of this chapter was presented at the 3rd 'International Single Session Therapy and Walk-in Services Symposium' entitled 'Single Session Thinking: Going Global, One Step at a Time' on 24 and 25 October 2019, in Melbourne, Australia. This earlier version was first published as Dryden, W. (2021). Sign up, meet up, speak out: Single sessions in the context of meetup groups. In. M.F. Hoyt, J. Young & P. Rycroft (eds), *Single Session Thinking and Practice in Global, Cultural and Familial Contexts: Expanding Applications* (pp. 153–62). Routledge. It appears here in an updated form with the kind permission of the publisher.

Behaviour Therapy and Coaching (CBT) and Rational Emotive Behaviour Therapy and Coaching (REBT). Everyone was welcome. People paid a £20 entry fee which covered the hire of the room and related expenses.

At each meeting, attended by about 50 people, I gave a presentation on a psychological theme, followed by two single sessions with volunteers from the audience. Each evening ran for two hours, usually 7–9 pm with a 15-minute intermission.

The work I did in the lectures and sessions had three functions. First, it had an educational function. It was a form of psychological education where people could learn about a problematic psychological issue (see Tables 6.2 and 6.3 below) and how it could be tackled from a CBT perspective. Second, it had a therapeutic function. Two people per evening entrusted me with their problems, and I wanted to be as helpful as possible while being mindful that they were discussing these problems in a public setting. Third, it had an entertainment function. My goal was to hold the attention of everyone in the room, and to this effect, I introduced humour as much as I could into my lectures and sessions while preserving the seriousness of the work. In what follows, I will focus on the single-session work that I did rather than on the lectures that I gave.

The Single Sessions

The single sessions that I did in these meetup group evenings followed the tradition of the public demonstrations carried out by Alfred Adler and Albert Ellis. From 1965 to 2015, Ellis carried out live demos of REBT in New York in what was called the 'Friday Night Workshop' (Ellis & Joffe, 2002) which continues to this day under the name 'Friday Night Live' (FNL) with sessions run by leading therapists at the Albert Ellis Institute. The format remains the same, however, with two volunteers from the audience being helped with their 'problems in living.' Lectures are not given at FNL.

Getting a Volunteer

When people signed up for a UK CBT meeting, they were asked if they were interested in volunteering as clients. At the meeting,

I stressed that a volunteer should have a problem relevant to the lecture topic that they were keen to address and willing to do so in front of the audience. Preference was given to someone who had not volunteered before.

Dealing with the Volunteer and the Audience

Before I started, I asked the audience to abide by the ethical rule, 'What is seen and heard here, stays here.' I asked them to observe silence during the sessions and stressed that they would be able to ask the volunteer and me any questions that they wished after the session.

I asked the volunteer permission to record the session, and they were sent the recording and transcript afterward on request. If the volunteer needed aftercare, I would make some recommendations to them. However, I never needed to do this in the 107 demonstrations I conducted in the life of the UK CBT meetup group. A few people volunteered more than once for help with different problems. Table 6.1 presents information about the first 100 sessions that I conducted and session timings.

Table 6.1   The first 100 single sessions in the UK CBT
Meetup: Session times

- From 28/6/12 to 25/10/18
- 74 females and 26 males

The average time of the session was 16 minutes 31 seconds

Session times ranged from 5 minutes 16 seconds to 29 minutes 46 seconds

- From 5 minutes to 9 minutes 59 seconds...5 sessions
- From 10 minutes to 14 minutes 59 seconds.. 35 sessions
- From 15 minutes to 19 minutes 59 seconds...40 sessions
- From 20 minutes to 24 minutes 59 seconds...15 sessions
- From 25 minutes to 29 minutes 59 seconds...5 sessions

Problems Discussed by Volunteers

At the outset, it is important to realise that the problems discussed by the volunteers reflected the themes of the lectures that I gave.

Tables 6.2 and 6.3 list the problems raised by volunteers by gender.

Table 6.2 Problems discussed by volunteers by gender

Problem	Female	Male
Anger	8	4
Anxiety & Phobia	10	2
Uncertainty	4	2
Lack of Control	4	1
Procrastination	17	4
Relationship Problems	5	3
Self-Esteem Problems	12	2
Other Emotional Problems	14	8
Total	**74**	**26**

How I Worked in These Demonstration Sessions
In this part of the chapter, I want to explain how I worked during the demonstration sessions. While I will outline a template of the way I worked, not all points that I cover were present in all the demonstration sessions. What I did depended on the time available, the nature of the problem brought by the volunteers, and what they wanted to achieve from the session.

Table 6.3 Other emotional problems by gender

Problem	Female	Male
Guilt	3	2
Shame	3	3
Hurt	4	2
Jealousy	2	0
Envy	1	1
Obsessive-Compulsive Disorder	1	0
Total	**14**	**8**

My main orientation is Rational Emotive Behaviour Therapy to which I bring a single-session mindset (see Dryden, 2019 and Chapter 7 in this volume). Both the volunteer and I proceeded, knowing that the session that we would have would be our only therapeutic encounter. A possible referral was not discussed at the outset. About 5% of the volunteers asked me later if I could recommend a therapist with whom they could take things further, which I did. I never recommended myself. However, the volunteer knew that I would send them, on request, an audio copy of the session and, later, a transcript of the session for subsequent review. Approximately 70% of volunteers emailed me to request a copy of the recording and transcript.

Selecting the Issue

At the very beginning of the session, I asked the volunteer what issue they wanted to address with me. If they mentioned more than one issue, I asked them to select *one* which to which I refer to as the 'nominated issue'. I then helped the person to formulate this issue.

Establishing a Goal-Orientation

I then adopted a goal orientation with the volunteer. Here, it is important to distinguish between a *problem-related goal* – what the volunteer wanted to achieve concerning the nominated issue and *a session goal* – what the person wanted to achieve by the end of the session.

I encouraged the volunteer to see that the achievement of a session goal was a stepping stone to achievement of a problem-related goal. This fitted in well with how I see the objectives of SST which are to (i) help the client address a specific issue; (ii) to help the client get 'unstuck' and (iii) to help the client take a few steps forward which may help them to travel the rest of the journey without professional assistance (Dryden, 2024a).

Understanding Past Attempts at Dealing with the Issue

As is common practice in SST, I ascertained how the volunteer had tried to deal with the issue in the past and what was the outcome of these attempts. I encouraged the volunteer to distance themself from unhelpful components of these attempts and capitalize on helpful components.

Dealing with a Specific Example of the Nominated Issue, if Relevant

If the client's nominated issue lent itself to the examination of a specific example, then I helped them to select such an example. In doing so, I wanted to discover specific information concerning who was present, what happened, and where it happened. While the chosen example could be recent, typical or vivid, I often encouraged the volunteer to select one that was imminent, if relevant. The value of a future example was that the work done on it lent itself to the implementation of any solution chosen by the volunteer.

Assessing the Specific Example: The Situational ABC Model

When I worked with a specific example of the volunteer's nominated issue, I assessed it using the 'Situational *ABC* Model' that stems from Rational Emotive Behaviour Therapy (REBT). Briefly, this model states that when a problem occurs, it does so

in a situational context. Here, the person responds unconst-
ructively (at *C*) to a feature of the situation, which is an adversity
(at *A*) for them. The core of the REBT model is that these
unconstructive responses are best explained by the rigid and
extreme basic attitudes (at *B*) the person holds towards the
adversity. REBT argues that the person's best solution to their
nominated issue is to develop an alternative set of flexible and
non-extreme basic attitudes (at *B*) towards the adversity (at *A*).
This will result in them dealing with the adversity in a more
constructive manner (at *C*). This is summarised in Table 6.4.
Please note that I did not use this framework explicitly or
formally with the volunteer. Rather, I kept it in mind while
assessing the nominated issue and planning interventions.

Table 6.4 REBT's *Situational ABC* Framework

Situation =	Description of context	
A =	Adversity (The aspect of situation to which the person responds emotionally, cognitively and behaviourally)	
B =	Basic attitude (Rigid/Extreme or Flexible/Non-Extreme)	
C [e] =	Emotional consequence (Healthy or Unhealthy)	
[t] =	Thinking consequence (Negative and Highly Distorted or Balanced and Realistic)	
[b] =	Behavioural consequence (Dysfunctional or Functional)	

The following steps, which are notional rather than fixed, should
help to clarify what happened during such an assessment.

Step 1: Situation. Here, I got a brief description of the situation
in which the episode occurred.

Step 2: Emotional C. Here, I identified the person's most

troublesome negative emotion and the behaviour and thinking that accompanied it, if necessary.

Step 3: Adversity. I was then ready to identify the aspect of the situation that the volunteer was most troubled about. This represented the adversity at *A*. At this point, I encouraged the person to assume temporarily that the adversity had happened. Even if the adversity could have been shown to be inaccurate, the point was that the person responded to it as if it were true, and thus, we proceeded on that basis, but only if doing so made sense to the person. If not, I took a different tack. In Table 6.5 (see next page), I outline the most efficient way that I have found of identifying *A* if this was not clear at the outset.

Step 4: Adversity-based goal. Before I proceeded to help the volunteer understand the role that their attitudes played in both their problem and the potential solution to their problem, I helped them to set a realistic adversity-based goal. This involved me helping them to see that they could still have an emotion that felt bad but was healthy and was at the heart of a constructive response to the adversity (e.g. concern rather than anxiety about facing a threat). Identifying such a goal helped me when I took an attitudinal focus.

Step 5: Identifying basic attitudes. I next shifted focus and helped the volunteer understand the role of rigid/extreme basic attitudes at *B* played in their problem and the potential role that flexible/non-extreme basic attitudes had in the solution to their problem. This would be the same as their adversity-based goal identified above. In Table 6.6 (see p. 159), I outline the most efficient way that I have found in doing this work.

Identifying the Solution

By now, it should be clear that REBT offers the volunteer an attitude-based solution to their target issue. In short, if the person developed and acted on a set of flexible and non-extreme attitudes towards adversity, they would achieve their problem-related goal. If the volunteer accepted this, then we proceeded to the next step. If not, I helped them develop a non-attitude-based solution.

Table 6.5 Windy's Magic Question (WMQ)

The purpose of this technique is to help the volunteer to identify the *A* in the *ABC* framework as quickly as possible (i.e. what the person is most disturbed about) once *C* has been assessed and the situation in which *C* has occurred has been identified and briefly described

- **Step 1:** I have the person focus on their disturbed *C* (e.g. 'anxiety')
- **Step 2:** I then ask the person to focus on the situation in which *C* occurred (e.g. 'about to give a public presentation to a group of consultants')
- **Step 3:** I then ask the person, "Which ingredient could we give you that would eliminate or significantly reduce *C*? (here, anxiety)? (In this case, the person said, 'my mind not going blank'). I take care that the person does not change the situation (i.e. that they do not say: 'not giving the presentation')
- Step 4: The opposite to this ingredient is probably *A* (e.g. 'my mind going blank'), but I check this. Thus, I ask, 'So when you were about to give the presentation, were you most anxious about your mind going blank?' If not, I use the question again until the person confirms what they were most anxious about in the described situation

---

Implementing the Solution

The first step to help the person implement an attitude-based solution was for me to encourage them to strengthen the flexible/non-extreme attitudes that they had chosen (see above). I did this in a variety of ways in the session. These included:

- Asking them to imagine teaching their selected attitude to their loved ones;
- Helping them to identify and respond to any doubts, reservations or objections they have about their selected attitude;
- Encouraging them to engage in attitude-based, in-session practice of the solution (e.g. through role-play, imagery and chair-work).

Table 6.6 Windy's Review Assessment Procedure (WRAP)

Once *C* (e.g. 'anxiety') and *A* (e.g. 'my mind going blank') have been assessed, I often use this technique to identify both the person's client's rigid/extreme and flexible/non-extreme basic attitudes and help the person to understand the two relevant *B-C* connections.

• **Step 1:** I begin by saying, 'Let's review what we know and what we don't know so far'

• **Step 2:** I then say, 'We know three things. First, we know that you were anxious (*C*). Second, we know that you were anxious about your mind going blank (*A*). Third, and this is an educated guess on my part, we know that it is important to you that your mind does not go blank. Am I correct?' Assuming that the person confirms my hunch, what I have done is to identify the part of the attitude that is common to both the person's rigid attitude and alternative flexible attitude

• **Step 3:** I continue by saying, let's review what we don't know. This is where I need your help. We don't know which of two attitudes your anxiety was based on. So, when you were anxious about your mind going blank was your anxiety based on Attitude Number 1: 'It is important to me that my mind does not go blank and therefore it must not do so' ('Rigid attitude') or Attitude Number 2: 'It is important to me that my mind does not go blank, but that does not mean that it must not do so ("Flexible attitude")?'

• **Step 4:** If necessary, I help the person to understand that their anxiety was based on their rigid attitude if they are unsure.

• **Step 5:** Once the person is clear that their anxiety was based on their rigid attitude, I make and emphasize the rigid/extreme attitude-disturbed *C* connection. Then, I ask 'Now let's suppose instead that you had a strong conviction in attitude number 2, how would you feel about your mind going blank if you strongly believed that while it was important to you that your mind did not go blank, it did not follow that it must not do so?'

• **Step 6:** If necessary, I help the person nominate a healthy negative emotion such as concern, if not immediately volunteered, and make and emphasize the flexible/non-extreme attitude-healthy *C* connection.

Helping the Volunteer Understand the Change Process

I found it useful to outline a realistic view of the change process with the volunteer. This included the importance of rehearsing healthy attitudes, and regularly acting in ways that are consistent with this developing attitude.

Helping the Volunteer to Develop a Cognitive-Behavioural Plan

With the above points in mind, my next step was to help the person develop a cognitive-behavioural plan to implement their selected solution. This involved them being clear with themself how they could best integrate the solution in their life and when, where and how frequently they were prepared to implement this plan.

Ending

As with other forms of single-session therapy, it is important to have a good ending (Hoyt & Rosenbaum, 2018). I did this by encouraging the person to summarise what they were going to take away from the session and to voice any last-minute issue or ask any questions they might have wished they had asked me once they had gotten home.

Audience Input

Once the session had finished, I invited members of the audience to ask myself and the volunteer suitable questions or make any relevant observations as they saw fit. My role here was to encourage discussion and to preserve what the volunteer would take away from the session. Questions encompassed both the session's content and the intervention's process. This format could conceivably be used widely in the training of single-session therapists.

Clinical Example

'Eloise' (not her real name) was a woman in her mid-40s who volunteered for help at a meetup group where the theme was 'Dealing with Anxiety'. The following is an edited transcript of the highlights of the interview. The dots indicate missing conversation.

Selecting the Issue

Windy:　　What problem can I help you with this evening?

Eloise:　　I get worried and anxious if my 18-year-old son comes home late from college or from a night out.

Windy:　　What do you do when you're worried?

Eloise:　　I keep calling in on the phone...

Establishing a Goal-Orientation

Windy:　　What would you like to take away from the session that would give you a sense that you were glad you volunteered this evening?

Eloise:　　A way of not worrying...

(I return to the issue of goals later.)

Understanding Past Attempts at Dealing with the Issue

Windy:　　What have you done in the past to address the problem?

Eloise:　　I have tried to distract myself or do what I do now, which is to phone him when he is five minutes late.

Windy:　　What effect have these two methods had on you?

Eloise:　　They help me in what you called in the lecture 'the short term' but not in the longer term...

Dealing with a Specific Example of the Nominated Issue, if Relevant

Windy:　　When is your son next going to college or going out?

Eloise: He has a week off from college, but he is going out with his mates tomorrow night.

Windy: Do you anticipate having the problem tomorrow?

Eloise: For sure, if he is late.

Assessing the Specific Example: The Situational ABC Model

Windy: Let's assume that he will be late, shall we? (*Situation*).

Eloise: OK.

Windy: What would you be worried about? (Emotional *C* = worry – see above)

Eloise: That he will be harmed in some way...........

Windy: What one ingredient would take your worry away?

Eloise: Knowing he is safe...

Windy: So, are you most worried about not knowing that he is safe?

Eloise: Yes (*A* = not knowing that my son is safe).

Windy: So, we know that you are worried and that you would prefer to know that he is safe. But we don't know what your attitude towards this uncertainty is when you are worried. Shall we find out?

Eloise: Yes, please.

Windy: Is it, attitude 1, 'I want to know that my son is safe and therefore I absolutely must know this' or attitude 2, 'I want to know that my son is safe, but I don't absolutely have to have this certainty'? Which attitude is your worry based on?

Eloise: Put like that, definitely number 1 (Rigid basic attitude at B = 'I want to know that my son is safe and therefore I absolutely must know this')...

Clarifying the Adversity-Based Goal and Identifying a Solution

Windy: And how would you feel if you really believed attitude number 2? (Potential solution = Flexible basic attitude at B = 'I want to know that my son is safe but I don't have to have this certainty').

Eloise: I'm not sure of the word for it but my worry would be manageable.

Windy: Remember in the lecture, I distinguished between worry and worry-free concern?

Eloise: Yes, but for me as a Jewish mother I need to see myself worry.

Windy: So, how about manageable worry rather than unmanageable worry? (Adversity-based goal)
Eloise: Perfect

I then helped Eloise to anchor the following constructive behaviours with her new flexible basic attitude (a) asking her son to call her if he was going to be late; (b) calling him 45 minutes after he was expected home if he forgot to call; (c) not checking her phone in the interim period even if she felt the urge to do so; and (d) getting on with whatever she would be doing if she knew he was safe.

I then took her through an imagery rehearsal of these components, and she agreed to implement this cognitive-behavioural plan in imagery twice a day and whenever her son was late. I ended by asking her to review the session from her perspective and see if she had any questions or points to make. I then asked the audience for their comments and questions.

Postscript

After COVID-19, the world had moved on. Online training events in psychotherapy and counselling had become the norm, and there was little interest in in-person events such as we ran at the UK CBT meetup group. Consequently, the group folded. However, I began to offer weekly online REBT-based demonstrations (without accompanying lectures) for the REBT Facebook group. I did 176 such demonstrations between late 2020 and early 2024 (see Dryden, 2021b).

7

Capturing and Making Use of the Moment: REBT-Informed Single-Session Therapy

Abstract

In this chapter,[31] I discuss how well the ideas that inform the practice of single-session therapy (SST) fit with those that inform the practice REBT. I then outline what an REBT-informed single-session therapy looks like in practice (Dryden, 2019) and present a transcript (with commentary) of a single session of REBT-informed SST.

What is Single-Session Therapy?

As I outlined in Chapter 1, single-session therapy (SST) is an intentional endeavour where therapist and client agree to work together to see if the latter can help the client deal with their problem in one session, knowing that more help is available if needed or wanted (Dryden, 2020, 2024a), There are occasions when the REBT therapist might only have one session with a person. First, the client may state at the outset that for whatever reason, they just want to have one session of therapy. In this case,

---

[31] Keynote address read at the 4th International Congress on REBT, Cluj, Romania, 13–15 September 2019. The original title was 'Look, if you had one shot or one opportunity to seize everything you ever wanted in one moment. Would you capture it or just let it slip?: Single-session REBT. This was published as Dryden (2022). Capturing and making use of the moment: REBT-informed single-session therapy. In W. Dryden (ed.), *New Directions in Rational Emotive Behaviour Therapy* (pp. 55–76). Routledge. This chapter is an updated version and appears here with the kind permission of the publisher.

if the therapist chooses to proceed, then it will be done on that basis. Second, when an REBT therapist does a demonstration then that will be the only time that they will meet with the person (see Chapter 3). Albert Ellis used to do such demonstrations at his Friday Night Workshops and during his training courses and did so throughout his career. Incidentally, even in his therapy sessions, Albert Ellis practised REBT without assuming that a client would return.

Reasons Why SST Is Offered

There are several reasons why therapy agencies offer single-session therapy to clients as part of their service delivery. First, SST reflects how many clients behave when making use of therapeutic services. Thus, data collected from public and non-profit therapy agencies from around the world show that the modal number of sessions people have is '1' (Brown & Jones, 2005; Hoyt & Talmon, 2014; Young, 2018). Data also show that between 70% and 80% of those who have a single session are satisfied with it given their current circumstances (Hoyt & Talmon; 2014; Talmon, 1990). Also, about 50% of these single-session clients do not require further help after the session (Young, 2018).

However, perhaps the most compelling reason why SST is offered is that it is based on providing help at the point of need rather than at the point of availability. Public and non-profit agencies tend to struggle with waiting lists and try to solve this problem by offering 'blocks' of therapy sessions which are relatively unsuccessful. By contrast, SST both meets the needs of clients who want a rapid response to a pressing concern and reduces both waiting lists and waiting time.

The Goals of SST

As I made clear earlier in the chapter, SST is purposive and the goals of the therapist can be divided into outcome goals and process goals.

Outcome Goals

The single-session therapist recognises that different clients want to get different things from the session and endeavours to find out what this is at the outset. Some clients may seek emotional relief and hope to gain a sense of hope from speaking with a therapist, while others may wish to seek specific help for pressing concerns with which they have become 'stuck'. Sometimes being helped to take a few steps forward may help the client to deal with the problem. which may help them to travel the rest of the journey without professional assistance. Aside from helping the client to deal effectively with a pressing emotional concern, the therapist may be called upon to help the client deal with a dilemma or make an important decision.

Process Goals

Process goals are those that are designed to help the client achieve their outcome goals. They are to be achieved in the session in contrast to outcome goals, which are to be achieved after the session. One major process goal involves the therapist helping the client to identify a workable solution to their nominated concern which they might rehearse in the session, if possible. Such a solution may involve the client changing their perspective or their behaviour. Another important process goal involves the therapist helping the client to identify internal and external resources that they may use in implementing their solution. The final process goal that I will mention concerns the therapist helping the client to develop an action plan which will aid them in the implementation of their solution.

The Single-Session Mindset in Action

Single-session therapy is not an approach to therapy. Rather, it is a way of delivering services and a mindset which therapists bring to the work. Thus, SST can be practised by therapists from a variety of therapeutic orientations, including, of course REBT. However, what is important is the presence of the single-session mindset when SST is carried out. This mindset has the following features which all have practical implications.

1. Since it cannot be known with any degree of certainty that a client will return for a second session, the SST practitioner works on the assumption that this may be the only session that they may have with the client. As such, the therapist works with the client to help them fully to address their nominated concern in the session on the understanding that further help is available to the client, if needed and wanted.

2. The therapist creates a realistic expectation of what can be achieved in the session, detailing, if appropriate, what they can do and what they can't do.

3. The therapist encourages the client to specify what they would like to walk away with at the end of the session.

4. The therapist and the client agree on a focus for the session and the therapist helps the client to keep on track.

5. As noted above, the therapist adopts a resources-based focus, helping the client to identify and utilise inner strengths and helpful aspects of their environment while addressing their nominated concern.

6. Having understood the nominated concern, the therapist invites the client to use all relevant information to select the most feasible solution to this concern and to rehearse this solution in the session. The therapist then helps the client to develop an action plan to implement the solution.

7. The therapist encourages the client to summarise the session and to articulate what they are going to take away from it. Then the therapist encourages the client to spend some time implementing their learning from the session reminding them that after this period they can access further help, if needed. The therapist then ends the session on a good note, if possible.

Good Practice in SST and the REBT Perspective

In this section, I will discuss what is considered to be good practice in SST and outline the REBT perspective on each point.

As will be seen, in my view shown there is a high degree of consistency between the two therapeutic areas.

Agreeing the Objective of the Session

At the beginning of the session, the single-session therapist comes to an agreement with the client concerning the objective of their meeting and the therapist makes clear, if necessary, what they can do and what they can't do. This represents the value that REBT places on *explicitness* and it is certainly something that most REBT therapists would do at the beginning of therapy.

Engaging the Client Quickly by Getting Down to Work

The single-session therapist engages the client quickly through the work that they do from the outset. The SST practitioner does not do a lengthy assessment of the client, conduct a case history or carry out a case formulation because engaging in these activities are not necessary for the conduct of SST and if engaged in would make the session inordinately long without providing additional benefit for either therapist or client. This is consistent with REBT's 'let's get down to business' problem-focused approach. After asking his clients a few standard biographical questions, Ellis would in the first five minutes of his first session with a client ask the client what problem they wanted to discuss with him and begin therapy with them at that point. In my view, this makes REBT and SST a perfect marriage on this point.

Adopting a Prudently Active Stance

The single-session therapist is prudently active during the session while taking care to encourage the client to be active. The REBT therapist is active in their use of Socratic questioning which invites the client to be actively involved in this dialogue. Even when the REBT therapist is didactic at various junctures they ensure the involvement by asking the client to summarise the points that are being put to them and to voice their doubts, reservations and objections to any of these points (see later).

Being Solution-Focused or Problem/Solution-Focused

An SST practitioner is either solution-focused or problem/solution-focused. The latter elicits the client's nominated problem from their perspective before helping them to understand the factors involved in this problem (problem assessment) and thence to find a solution based on that understanding. In REBT, a distinction is made between a client's 'problem-as-experienced' and their 'problem-as-assessed', a viewpoint that is consistent with the practice of problem/solution-focused SST practitioners.

Focusing on Goals

The SST practitioner is focused at the outset on helping the client to achieve an end of session goal and to this end the therapist helps the client stay focused as well. However, the single-session therapist may also want to discover what goal the client has in mind with respect to their nominated problem and to make a connection between the problem-related goal and the end-of-session goal. Typically, the latter is seen as leading to the former. Ellis (1989) was sceptical of the REBT therapist asking their client for an end-of-session goal, arguing that this was a case of the therapist foisting on the client a goal that they do not have. However, Ellis's views were related to ongoing therapy and not to SST. Having said that in his single-session REBT demonstrations, Ellis would not ask the client for an end-of-session goal.

In general, the REBT therapist tends to use the *ABCDE* framework to help focus themself and their client, on the latter's nominated problem and problem-related goal. In particular, the REBT therapist would work towards helping the client set a goal with respect to the main adversity that features in their nominated problem. While the REBT therapist would tend not to ask a client for an end-of-session goal, there is nothing in the theory that would rule out this practice and I certainly ask for such a goal as an REBT-informed single-session therapist (see session transcript below).

Being Clear

The SST practitioner values clarity in all matters. In particular, they are clear about the nature of SST and what they can do and what they can't do. They also strive to ensure client understanding and agreement throughout the session. Finally, they are clear about the availability of further help and if that is the case how the client can access it and they explain their interventions and the rationale behind them, whenever practicable

The REBT therapist strives to be clear with the client and is especially keen to ensure that the clients understands key REBT concepts. Being clear is another example of *explicitness* which is again consistent with REBT practice.

Selecting an Agreed Focus

Time is of the essence in SST and thus, the therapist's main job is to help the client select a focus that is meaningful for them. Most often this will be a pressing concern that has been on the client's mind. While the therapist's main task is to help the client to deal with this concern, they will also look for ways to encourage the client to generalise their learning from the nominated problem to other areas of their life.

The REBT therapist would begin REBT by focusing on the client's nominated problem and would look later help the client to generalise what they learned from dealing with their specific problems to other issues. However, this would usually not be in the first session.

Adopting a Strengths-Based Approach

The single-session practitioner does not have the time to help a client to learn skills that are not already in their repertoire and therefore the therapist needs to help the client identify and bring to the session what they consider to be relevant strengths. This principle places SST squarely with what are known as the strengths-based therapies (Murphy & Sparks, 2018).

Although there is no formally acknowledged approach that might be called 'Strengths-based REBT', this strengths-based SST principle is not inconsistent with REBT.

Encouraging the Use of Environmental Resources

In addition to focusing on a client's strengths (i.e., internal resources), the SST practitioner will also encourage the client to identify and utilise relevant helping resources that are available to them in their environment (i.e. external resources). These may include supportive people in their life and organisations that may provide relevant assistance and guidance.

While the REBT therapist would largely help their client to identify and change internal factors, the flexible practice of REBT encompasses a dual focus on internal and external factors. It is both/and, not either/or. When the therapist cannot help a client to change internal factors, they will certainly help them, if possible, to change external factors.

Focusing on Previous Attempts to Solve Problems

The problem/solution-focused single-session therapist will ask their client to identify what attempts they have previously made to solve their problem. Having done so, they will help the client to build upon successful elements from these attempts and to cast aside those elements that were unsuccessful.

While the REBT therapist tends not to ask the client for their prior problem-solving strategies, this would not be deemed to be inconsistent with REBT practice.

Asking Questions

Most, but not all, SST practitioners make liberal use of questions during the session and this poses challenges for therapists who have trained not to as questions or to do so sparingly[32]. However, the liberal use of questions is quite consistent with how the REBT therapist practises.

---

[32] For therapists who think that they can't do SST without asking questions, I recommend viewing the famous Rogers/Gloria video which is, in effect, an example of SST: https://www.youtube.com/watch?v=ee1bU4XuUyg&t=686s accessed 27/08/24.

Dealing with Doubts, Reservations and Objections (DROs)

It is important that the client in SST leaves the session in a positive, optimistic frame of mind. To enable this to happen one of the things that the single-session therapist does is to encourage the client to identify and voice any doubts, reservations and objections (DROs) that they may have about any aspect of the session so that the therapist can respond to these DROs.

This practice is very consistent with what the REBT therapist strives to do when they encourage the client to express any DROs they may have about REBT concepts or the REBT therapeutic process.

Using Opportunities to Make an Emotional Impact

The single-session therapist strives to engage the client in a way that head and heart can work together thus helping ensure that the work has an emotional impact on the client. When this happens, it increases the chances that the client will take away something meaningful from the session. The therapist, therefore, seeks to avoid two things: (a) having a theoretical discussion with the client and (b) a situation where the client is so overwhelmed with emotions that they can't think. In both these situations, it is unlikely that the client will derive much benefit from the session.

The REBT therapist is aware of the importance of engaging clients emotionally in the work as there is a danger that discussions between the two can be overly intellectual. I have written on the need for the REBT therapist to guard against this and to make considered use of what I have called vivid therapeutic interventions (Dryden, 1986).

Refraining from Overloading the Client

The SST practitioner may want their client to take away as much as possible from the session given the fact that they may only be meeting once. In doing so, the therapist may unwittingly overload the client with many 'helpful' strategies and tips. The danger here is that the client may take away little of substance from the session. To guard against doing this the therapist encourages the client to take one meaningful point from the single session that they can apply in their life. This is enshrined in the SST principle, 'less is more'.

The above position is consistent with REBT. Given that REBT is an educational approach to therapy, the REBT therapist is mindful that their main goal is not to teach a client REBT concepts but to help them learn these concepts. Given this, a client learning one meaningful REBT concept in the session is better than them taking away four concepts, for example, poorly understood.

Searching for a Solution

Particularly, when the client nominates a specific problem, the single-session therapist strives to help the client take away a solution to this problem. Such a solution will reflect the strengths of the client, the successful elements of their previous attempts to deal with the problem and whatever concepts the therapist suggests to the client as potentially helpful.

The REBT therapist strives to help the client solve their problems by offering them an attitudinal solution. So, the solution-focused nature of REBT is consistent with the same focus in SST.

Rehearsing the Solution in the Session

Once the client has selected a solution, it is important for the SST practitioner to give them an opportunity to practise it in the session. This enables the client to get an experiential 'feel' of the solution to evaluate its potential helpfulness and to see if they think they can implement it in their life. Such rehearsal is entirely consistent with the practice of REBT.

Developing an Action Plan

Once the client has settled on a solution, the next step is for the single-session therapist to help them develop an action plan to implement the solution going forward. Such a plan will be general in nature, although the therapist might help the client select a specific way of 'kick-starting' the plan.

Being a cognitive-behavioural approach, REBT recommends the negotiation of specific homework assignments which can be reviewed at the following session. However, given the nature of SST, helping the client to develop an action plan is not inconsistent with REBT.

Ending the Session Well

If the client is to go away with a sense of optimism from the single session, it is important for the SST practitioner to help them end the session on a positive note. To ensure that this is done the therapist invites the client to ask any final questions or to tell the therapist anything that they wished they had told them once the session is concluded. Finally, the therapist reiterates that further help is available and how this help can be accessed, normally after the client has had a proper opportunity to implement their learning from the session and see if they need more help at that point.

While the above practices are not regularly done in REBT, they would not be inconsistent with REBT practice.

As can be seen from the above analysis there is much that is consistent between good practice in SST and what regularly happens in REBT. Taking this idea forward in the next section, I will outline what an REBT-informed approach to SST looks like.

The Practice of REBT-Informed Single-Session Therapy

The initial task of the REBT-informed single-session therapy practitioner is to agree with the client that they will meet for one session with the intention of helping the client achieve something meaningful that they can implement in their life knowing that more help is available if needed. If the client wishes to proceed on that basis, then the therapist and client will need to decide if there is time and willingness on behalf of the client to prepare for the session. If so, then such preparation can be done usually by the client completing a questionnaire which is shared with the therapist before the session.

At the beginning of the session, the therapist asks the client what they want to achieve by the end of the session and reminds the client that they are working together to help the client achieve that goal but that again more help is available if the client wants it in the future. This will usually be determined by the client once they have implemented what they learned from the session and allow time to pass to see what happens.

If the client wishes to discuss a specific emotional problem, the REBT-informed single-session therapist may help them to state their goal in line with the 'problem-as-experienced'. Then the therapist creates a focus that is centred on that problem and sets out to make an adversity-based assessment of this problem using the *Situational AC* part of the *Situational ABC* framework. Thus, the therapist asks for a specific example of the client's nominated problem, gets a description of the situation in which the problem occurred, identifies the client's main disturbed emotion (unhealthy negative emotion or UNE) at *C* and then identifies the adversity at *A*. In line with good REBT practice, the therapist then encourages the client to assume that this adversity is true. At this point the therapist helps the client to set an adversity-based goal in line with their 'problem-as assessed'.

Then, the therapist helps the client identify the rigid/extreme attitudes that underpin their emotional problem and encourages them to see that they have a choice between the one rigid/extreme attitude with which they identify as most responsible for their problem and its flexible/non-extreme attitudinal alternative. In doing so, the therapist helps the client see the relationship between this flexible/non-extreme attitude and their adversity-based goal.

Having underscored attitudinal choice, the therapist helps the client to examine both attitudes and to choose the one with which to proceed. This is normally the flexible/non-extreme attitude. This represents the 'solution' in SST-terms. The therapist then encourages the client to practise this attitude-based solution in the session by using such methods as imagery, role-play or chair-work.

Next, the REBT-informed single-session therapist outlines the change process for the client. This involves the client rehearsing their main flexible/non-extreme attitude, acting in ways consistent with this attitude and doing both of these things regularly over time. These activities are specified in an action plan agreed between therapist and client.

At appropriate times during the session, the therapist helps the client to identify their strengths, resiliency factors, values and external resources which they can draw upon during the session and afterwards as they implement their selected solution in their life.

Towards the end of the session the therapist encourages the client to summarise what they have learned from the session and plan to take forward into their own life. They are encouraged to ask any last-minute questions or to tell the therapist anything that they need to say before finishing so that they can leave with a sense of completeness and hope for the future. The therapist may then invite the client to engage in a process whereby they reflect and digest on what they have learned from the session, act on this learning and to see what happens before they decide whether or not to seek further help. Remember that SST does not preclude more help being available to the client.

Transcript of an REBT-Informed Single Session

The client, Nick, volunteered for a single session, knowing that this would be used as a demonstration for a course I run on single-session therapy. He has given written permission for this transcript to be used in this chapter and wanted me to use his real first name despite my offering to use a different name. My commentary on the session appears in brackets throughout the transcript.

Windy: Let me ask you, when you started to volunteer for this single session, what led you to do so?

[I begin this way because I wanted to know Nick's reasons for volunteering for the session.]

Nick: I've got an interest in REBT. I am doing a Master's degree at the moment. I changed careers recently and, in that career, I don't know, I have some issues with authority and..., I don't know, certain situations I find it very hard to communicate properly. I find myself, I don't know, not having the confidence to speak up and I can recognise some of the behaviours are just not helping me out. So, when I saw the opportunity to have a session with you, I jumped at it.

Windy: And, so, what would you hope to achieve by the end of the session?

[This is a typical SST 'goal at the end of the session' question.]

Nick: I'd love to feel more confident and keep my head up high when I do have conversations with certain people and, in meeting environments, feel more confident to speak up without feeling that I'm going to make a fool of myself.

[Note Nick's response. He has stated a goal that is not bounded by the end of the session. This is quite typical. Just because a therapist asks a clear question in SST it does not mean that the client will answer it as asked.]

Windy: And you hope to achieve that by the end of the session or do you hope to achieve that by putting into practice whatever we might talk about and that increased confidence might happen as a result of that?

[My response here is to 'layer' his goals and distinguish what he can realistically achieve in the single session and what this could lead to later.]

Nick: Yeah, I totally agree. I think it would definitely take some practice.

[Nick sees that there is a difference and notes that whatever he achieves by the end of the session will require practice.]

Windy: OK, because I think it's important for me to stress what I can do and what I can't do, and, however much I could give you confidence at the end of the session or you get confidence, the confidence will come from implementing whatever we decide that is going to be helpful to you. So, is there an example of this that might be coming up in the future that would be a good illustration of the problem that you can think about?

[*One of the tasks of the SST practitioner is to distinguish what they can do and what they cannot do. In doing so I reinforce Nick's point about implementation of 'whatever we decide is going to be helpful to you'. Note the words I use. I am emphasising the joint nature of our work. Also, note that I have asked for a future example for us to focus on. This is typical in SST and also good practice in REBT. It is easier to plan for change when one is working on a future example than when one works on a past example and then shifts the focus from the past to the future.*]

Nick: It's a little bit strange at the moment because I'm working from home. I could probably give you a past situation, if you want. Will that work?

Windy: Yeah. The reason I ask for a future one is because it's easier to gear what we talk about to the future. We can certainly look back, but we've still got to apply what you can glean from that past example to the future. But, if it makes sense to you to talk about, really, a good, clear example of that, that would be great.

Nick: Yeah. Well, I mean, there will be future ones. I do Skype meetings all the time and there's always one person in particular, when I find out I'm speaking to him, I do clam up and go a bit....

Windy: And are you going to be speaking to him?

Nick: Probably in the next couple of weeks there will be a high-level meeting which I'll have to speak in, yeah.

Windy: So, does it make sense to utilise him as an example?

[*Nick responds initially by offering a past example. By going with him it soon becomes clear that there*

*is a future example to be identified and I give my
rationale for working with it.*]

Nick: Yeah, definitely, if that's the way you want to go.
Yeah.

*[Nick responds by putting me in the driving seat
concerning the choice of example. I think he may be
a little bit 'REBT' star struck. Remember his phrase
earlier, 'So, when I saw the opportunity to have a
session with you, I jumped at it.' However, I want to
put him back in the driving seat which I do in my
next response.]*

Windy: Well, it's what's most helpful to you.

Nick: Yeah. I mean, I'd like to feel that I could go into one
of these higher-level meetings and feel a bit more
comfortable, definitely.

[Nick alludes to the future so I go with that.]

Windy: OK. So, let's imagine that you've got this Skype
meeting with this chap and what's the context?

*[I ask for the context to help us both understand the
situation in which his problem occurs. This is the
Situation in the Situational ABC framework.]*

Nick: Situational – I'm obviously working from home, on
a computer. I'm working on a major oil and gas
project at the moment. The gentleman in particular,
he's quite high up; he's at a manager's level. He's
quite a confident kind of person, quite cocky, he's
always butting in on the Skype calls and getting his
opinion going. So, basically, I work as what you call
a packer engineer instrumentation, so I have to give
my feedback on anything to do with that. So, I'm
called into the conversation quite a few times.

Windy: How many people on the Skype call?

Nick: It can be 10, it can be 30. It depends....

Windy: OK. But it's not just you and him, in other words?

Nick: No. It's in a group setting. Very rarely just me and him.

Windy: OK. So, in a couple of weeks, you'll come across this guy via Skype. Is that right?

Nick: That's correct, yeah.

Windy: And, so, what would the problem you think you might experience be like?

Nick: Well, as soon as I see he's on a call and as soon as I hear him speaking, I start getting a bit anxious – butterflies and I start clamming up.

Windy: What are you anxious about at that point?

[Having understood the context a little I ask for Nick's problem and he responds with anxiety. I then ask for what he is anxious about. In REBT terms, I have found the situation, and his major emotion in the situation (i.e. C), I have now asked about what he is anxious about which is known as an 'adversity' in REBT.]

Nick: ... I guess saying the wrong things. I'd like him to respect my opinion, but, I don't know, I'm not sure if I come across that way. I kind of clam up a little bit and underneath I realise that I do have the knowledge and I do have the experience, but, for some reason –

Windy: So, if you weren't anxious about saying the wrong thing, what would be different?

Nick: I guess I'd come across confident and not be so worried about speaking during these meetings.

Windy: OK. So, a number of dimensions there. One is that you mentioned about coming across confidently and the other thing is not saying something?

Nick: Not saying something stupid, really.

Windy: Not saying something stupid, OK. So, which of those two are the biggest threats for you? Coming across non-confidently or saying something stupid?

Nick: I think probably saying something. I mean, I guess it's not just stupid. It's saying something that's incorrect.

Windy: OK. So, saying something wrong.

Nick: Yeah, saying something wrong is probably the best.

Windy: OK. So, what's the biggest fear for you with this chap?

Nick: Probably that. Yeah, probably saying something that's wrong and being shot down for saying it.

Windy: OK. So, are you anxious about saying something wrong? Would you be anxious if you knew that you wouldn't be shot down?

Nick: ... [*Pause*] Yeah, I guess so.

Windy: You'd still be anxious about saying something wrong even if you knew that he wouldn't shoot you down?

[*In this sequence, I am asking Nick questions to find out what his adversity is which is the aspect of the situation that he is most anxious about. I employ a number of methods here: adding and subtracting elements, clarifying what I am hearing in his narrative.*]

Nick: Yeah, I think so. I guess it's about I want him to respect me, I guess. I kind of get these feelings when I speak in these meetings that they're talking behind my back once I've spoken, anyway. It might sound strange, but I feel like they do.

Windy: Saying what?

Nick: I don't know. Just putting me down or, 'He doesn't know anything.' I mean, I've come back; I had a 10-year break from this industry and I've come back into it and the confidence has gone a little bit. They know more than me, sort of thing.

Windy: OK. So, your basic anxiety is that you might say something incorrect?

[*From what I am hearing, this is Nick's adversity, and the other elements he has just mentioned are his cognitive elaborations that stem from his anxiety. In other words, they are cognitive Cs that stem from his rigid/extreme attitudes towards his adversity of saying something wrong in front of his boss.*]

Nick: I think so, yes.

[*Nick's response is not as definite as I would prefer and I could have picked up on his tentativeness here, But I choose to go with it and ask him in my next response for what I call an 'adversity-based goal'. This concerns how he would like to handle saying something incorrect in the meeting attended by his boss.*]

Windy: OK. Now, what would you like to achieve about the prospect of saying something incorrect?

Nick: ... Well, obviously, I'd like to say something –

Windy: Instead of being anxious about that, what would it be healthy for you to feel?

Nick: ... I guess knowing that, even if I do say something incorrect, then it's not the end of the world, I guess.

               [*Nick's response is interesting here and is probably coloured by his interest in REBT. Thus, he comes up with what is known in REBT as a 'non-awfulising attitude'.*]

Windy: And how would you feel if you believed that?

               [*Note my response. If he believed that, how would he feel? I know that he does not believe this, but I want to see if it is a viable solution. The only way I can do so is to have imagine him that he has conviction in that attitude to see what that would achieve.*]

Nick: ... I'd probably feel a lot calmer, a lot more comfortable.

Windy: Right, but you still wouldn't like it, would you?

Nick: No, definitely not. No. I want to come across as knowing what I'm supposed to know.

Windy: And, in advance, it sounds like you would still be concerned about the prospect of not saying anything incorrect.

Nick: Definitely, yeah. We all want to come across-

Windy: But you wouldn't be anxious?

Nick: I think if there isn't such a terrible side of things –
             thinking they're talking about me – no, I don't think
             I would be anxious. I think, if I could eliminate that,
             I would –

Windy: But you'd still be concerned?

Nick: Yes. Yeah.

Windy: OK.

             *[In this segment, I am working to help Nick see the
             difference between being concerned about saying
             something incorrect in front of his boss and being
             anxious about it. In doing this, I am attempting to
             link the realistic feeling of un-anxious concern, if
             you will, with his non-extreme attitude of not liking
             this, but it not being the end of the world.]*

Nick: Natural, yeah.

Windy: So, you mentioned that you have an interest in
             REBT, didn't you?

Nick: Yeah. I've been studying it in my Master's degree
             and I really like the sound of it.

Windy: Whereabouts?

Nick: 'X' University. I'm doing a distance Master's.

Windy: OK. So, from the point of view of what you know
             about REBT, how would you assess what your
             belief is, because we know what your feeling is,
             which is anxiety, and we know what you're anxious
             about, which is saying something incorrect, but
             what do you think your belief, or what I call your

attitude is that leads you to be anxious about saying something incorrect?

Nick: I guess I'm putting extreme pressure and demands on myself to always be correct; I must always have the correct answer to everything.

Windy: 'I must always have the correct answer.' Right, OK.

Nick: Yeah.

[*Picking up on Nick's interest in REBT, I feel more confident about using an REBT conceptualisation of his anxiety, here linking it to the rigid attitude that he expresses.*]

Windy: Now, have you tried to challenge that for yourself?

[*Since Nick has expressed an interest in REBT, I want to determine if he has had any prior experience in challenging his rigid attitude so that I can build on skills that he has.*]

Nick: Not particularly. I've tried it on a few other things, but not this particular one. I've saved this just for you.

Windy: You did? OK. That's very kind of you. But, if I was to ask you to utilise your skills in other areas to this particular one, what would it sound like?

[*Nick has had some experience of examining his rigid/extreme attitudes and so I ask him to transfer these skills to the present situation and attitude.*]

Nick: Well, I need to create a more rational view that it's OK to be wrong. It's not the end of the world. I'm not, as I've worded it, a stupid person if I do get things wrong.

Windy: Right. And how about the 'must'? How would you challenge the 'must'?

Nick: ... Well, I mean ... just because I think I must, it doesn't mean it's right, it doesn't mean it's true.

Windy: Right.

Nick: And, obviously because I'm exhibiting not very helpful behaviours when I am in this situation, hopefully, by changing from a 'must' to a more rational, flexible viewpoint, then, hopefully, I'll-

Windy: And what will that viewpoint be with respect to saying something incorrect?

Nick: ... It would just be I would like to be right but I don't have to be right.

Windy: Right, OK. So, if you bring all that together and you rehearse the idea that, 'I'd like to be right. I don't have to be. It's not the end of the world and I'm still,' what? What's your attitude about yourself going to be under those circumstances?

Nick: I guess, in a work context, I'm still a valuable employee that has lots to give, I guess.

Windy: Yeah. And that you can still accept yourself whether you say things incorrect or not, would be the additional thing, wouldn't it?

Nick: Yeah, definitely.

[From an REBT perspective, Nick's anxiety is based on a rigid attitude ('I have to be right') and two extreme attitudes that stem from this rigid attitude, 'It's the end of the world if I'm not right' (awfulising attitude) and 'I'm a stupid person if I'm not right'

(self-devaluation attitude). His concern is based on a flexible attitude ('I'd like to be right, but I don't have to be right') and two non-extreme attitudes, 'It's not the end of the world if I'm not right (non-awfulising attitude) and 'I'm still a valuable employee and can accept myself if I say things that are incorrect or not' (unconditional self-acceptance attitude). Note that this latter attitude is half his contribution and half mine. This is the solution that will help Nick being concerned, but not anxious about being incorrect in the presence of his critical boss. I am now going to ask him to rehearse this solution to see if it sits well with him. I decide to take him through a guided imagery.]

Windy: OK. Now, could you imagine rehearsing that?

Nick: … [*Pause*] Yeah. Yeah, I think I could.

Windy: OK. So, let's take you through a rehearsal. You can do this with your eyes closed or eyes open. So, you're about to join a Skype call and you know that this chap's there and you start off being anxious because that's the usual way of the world. And then you say, 'Aha, I'm making myself anxious. I know what I'm anxious about. I'm anxious because I'm demanding that I mustn't say anything incorrect. No, I don't have to achieve that. I'm not a robot. There's always a possibility and, if I do, that will be unfortunate, and I can still accept myself. Even if he and others put me down, I can still accept myself.' Now, can you imagine rehearsing that?

[Note that in this guided imagery, I present the realistic possibility that he will begin by being anxious, but that he can use his anxiety to identify his rigid attitude respond to it with a flexible attitude and remind himself of brief versions of his non-awfulising and unconditional self-acceptance attitudes.]

Nick: Yeah, I think I could do that.

Windy: OK. Now, what do you think, if you took the same attitude about the idea that you'd like him to respect you, how would you deal with your anxiety about him not respecting you, utilising the same approach?

        [Maybe I am asking him to do too much work here, but I wanted to show how he could use this solution to another adversity that he mentioned at the outset – his boss's negative attitude towards him.]

Nick: … *[Pause]* Well, I guess I need to challenge, first of all, the demands that he must respect me. I need to … accept that, if he doesn't respect me- Well, I need to create an alternative belief, really, attitude.

Windy: Which would be what?

Nick: That I'd like the respect of my colleague. If he doesn't, then it's not the end of the world and I'm still a worthy person, I guess.

Windy: Yeah. You can still accept and respect yourself, even though he can't.

Nick: Yeah.

Windy: Now, let's imagine you really believe that, right? And let's compare your strong belief in that more flexible philosophy and we compare it to the rigid one that you currently hold about at least your anxiety. Which of those two philosophies leads to the idea that people are going to be talking behind your back and telling each other that you don't know what you're talking about? The idea that you must always say things correctly and you must get his respect or the idea that you don't always have to be correct and you don't always have to have respect? Which of those two belief systems are going to lead to that idea that people are talking about you negatively behind your back?

Nick: Definitely the first one, the one where I'm putting demands on myself.

Windy: That's right. Now, the second one you might still, 'Well, they might,' but then you also might think that they may not. So, in a sense, I think this shows how, nicely, that, when we have these rigid ideas, we're not only creating our anxiety – and the way you've been dealing with your anxiety, unfortunately and understandably, is the way of perpetuating it, because you've been dealing with it by staying silent.

Nick: Yeah.

Windy: Incidentally, when you stay silent, you're really saying, 'I'd better stay silent because, if I do say something stupid, then that will be terrible. So I'd better stay silent.'

Nick: Yeah.

Windy: But you, not only create your anxiety and your behaviour, which is to stay silent, also creates the idea, this picture of the world that other people are talking about you after the meeting and saying what a bloody dead loss you are.

[My goal in doing this piece of work is to help Nick see that his rigid/extreme attitudes leads him to make highly distorted inferences that are skewed to the negative and that if his attitudes were flexible/non-extreme these subsequent inference would be more balanced. I would not have done this

piece of work if he knew nothing about REBT and if we were not recording it. Knowing that he was going to get a recording and a transcript if the session later led me to take the risk. Overloading the client is a problem in SST and one that I am aware I have a tendency to do.]

Nick: Yeah.

Windy: You see?

Nick: Yeah, totally.

Windy: Now, do you have any doubts, reservations and objections to rehearsing these new ideas that we're talking about here?

Nick: No, not at all. I'd really like to become more confident in the workplace. So, no, I'll definitely give it a try.

Windy: Right, and my guess is, the more you practise these ideas and rehearse them, you can rehearse them – God has given us the power of imagination, so you could always go through the idea and practise it on a daily basis and certainly before you go into the meeting. And, the more you do that and the more you speak up – because, by staying silent, that's going to be a problem – the more confident you'll be and the more prepared you'll be if you do say something incorrect, because you might.

Nick: Yeah, definitely.

Windy: Do you know why you might?

Nick: ... Because there's no guarantee I'll always be right.

Windy: Yes, unless you're a programmed robot.

Nick: Yeah.... That makes a lot of sense. Yeah.

Windy: OK. So, is there anything else about this that we need to talk about?

Nick: ... I don't think so. I think that was the gist of it. I think rehearsing it's a good thing. I think it will help me out a lot. Yeah.

              [*Developing an action plan with a client does not have to be elaborate. The main point is that Nick needs to rehearse his solution which he does seem to grasp.*]

Windy: Now, could you generalise this to any other areas of your life? These ideas that we're talking about, are they generalisable to other areas of your life?

              [*My thinking at the time was that I wanted to help Nick to see if he could generalise this solution to other areas of his life. We have dealt with the two adversities in his work problem – his anxiety about saying something wrong and his anxiety about the manager not respecting his opinion. Now I see if there is another life arena where he can apply his solution. Again, I raise the question about whether I am overloading him.*]

Nick: I think so. I'm not the most confident of people. I can be confident, but I'd describe myself as not the most social, and I really want to be social with friends.

Windy: So, give me an idea how you can practise this new philosophy in a social arena?

Nick: Well, when you're in groups of people, there's always someone who's stronger, and I have this tendency just to let them speak. So, I think I could practise it a lot more in that environment and try and be a bit more confident, and accept that –

Windy: And accept that what?

Nick: And just accept that I'm going to say something silly sometimes, but it's not the end of the world. I'm still me.

Windy: Right.

Nick: I'm still worthy.

Windy: 'And, if they take the mickey out of me,' what?

[*Here, I provide an adversity for him to grapple with.*]

Nick: Then it's up to them. It's not my problem. I'm happy with who I am.

Windy: Yeah, although you'd prefer them not to take the mickey out of you.

[*The 'it's not my problem' response leads me to reiterate the flexible attitude that he would prefer others not to 'take the mickey out of him'.*]

Nick: Of course, yeah.

Windy: Yeah, OK. So, the point is that this philosophy, although we're talking about it with your boss and in terms of authority. So, tell me a little bit – I am interested about this idea of authority. Have you had problems with authority going back in your life?

[*I am testing a hunch here, but it turns out that I'm wrong. No harm done, I think?*]

Nick: I don't think so. I've moved around a lot. When I was younger, I moved around a lot. I never had much stability in schools and stuff; I went to a lot of schools. So, I guess I never had a chance to actually build my self-confidence in social environments. So, I think maybe it stems from that. I'm not sure. But not particularly. In my previous experience in the oil industry, I never wanted to progress, I never took the opportunities, again because I guess I didn't feel comfortable with my own abilities.

Windy: Right. So, you've basically reacted to being uncomfortable and not confident by playing safe.

Nick: In the work environment, yeah.

Windy: Yeah.

Nick: … Yeah. I mean, I've got a tendency to not stop. I like to continuously educate myself, try a new thing all the time. So, I think that might be my reaction to feeling I'm not worthy or I'm not at a high educational level.

Windy: But it sounds like now you are; you're doing a Master's. Is it an online Master's that you're doing?

Nick: Yeah, it's a distance. We're meant to visit now and again, but, yeah, it's predominantly distance.

Windy: And do you experience this issue on the course?

Nick: Not at all. I've absolutely immersed myself in it and love it. It's really something that's appealed to me for a long time.

Windy: OK.

Nick: Again, there's not much communication between people.

[*I am not very happy with this segment of the session. It does not really go anywhere and I run the risk of reducing the impact from the work Nick and I did earlier. So, I decide to bring the focus back and ask Nick to summarise the session.*]

Windy: OK. So, why don't you summarise the work that we've done today?

Nick: So, first of all we discussed and highlighted the problem. We found a specific example of a future instance of when I may feel anxious and we highlighted that the issues are probably stemming from the fact that I'm placing demands on myself to be correct in every situation in the workplace and maybe outside the workplace. So, to dispute that, we looked at the alternative, more flexible attitude and belief that we want to take and, by practising and rehearsing that using imagery prior to the events, hopefully, over time, that will help me develop more rational beliefs, which should, hopefully, change from anxious to concern, and accepting myself no matter what happens.

Windy: Yeah. The more you do it, the more you get the benefit, and what will happen to your level of confidence?

[*Although the focus of the session has been on addressing Nick's anxieties, I do not forget that Nick began the session by wanting to be more confident and bring this topic into focus at this point.*]

Nick: I'm hoping my confidence in these environments will improve, yeah.

Windy: Yeah. Again, the more you do it with a healthier, flexible philosophy, my hypothesis is the more confident you will become.

[Note that I link his confidence with rehearsal of his flexible attitude.]

Nick: That will be great.

Windy: Yeah. So, is there anything that, if you went home and said, 'I wish I'd mentioned that today in the session,' or, 'I wish I'd asked that in the session', anything that you want to ask now so that you can leave with a sense of closure and this has been a good experience for you?

[The typical way to end a session in SST.]

Nick: ... *[Pause]* It's really quite hard to think.... *[Pause]* I'm not sure, really. I love the idea of just accepting yourself no matter the situation. We've gone with the rehearsal side of things. Is there anything for self-depreciation that you'd recommend for rehearsal or techniques to use for that?

Windy: Well, to recognise, I think, that there's a technique which you may know about – it's called The Big 'I', Little 'i' technique. The Big 'I', Little 'i' technique is that, when you say something incorrect, then that is a little 'i', and your big 'I' is composed of a whole multitude of these little 'i's and you may not like the fact that you've said something stupid, but it doesn't define you.

Nick: Yeah.

Windy: So, you might want to go home and draw a big 'I' like that and then put little 'i's in there and carry that around with you and say, 'Yeah, that is the bit of me that I've just revealed, I've just said something stupid, but does it define the whole of me?'

Nick: Yeah.

Windy: So, I might suggest that as an additional thing for you to take.

[Asking the client if there is anything that they want to say or ask before we close is always a risk. I use the opportunity to give Nick an additional way of addressing what he calls self-depreciation. Again, I wonder if I am overloading him.]

Nick: Yeah. I'll give that a try.

Windy: Alright. So, are we done?

Nick: I think so. I've found it very helpful.

Windy: Good. OK. Thank you very much and all the best, and thank you for allowing us to record this and to actually show it on the course.

Nick: No problem at all. Nice to meet you, Windy.

Windy: Take care. Bye-bye.

8

What's in a Name?
What to Call Therapy Where a Client
May Come Once

In 1990, an Israeli psychologist, Moshe Talmon, published a book that would herald a way of working with people therapeutically and would challenge conventional ways of thinking about therapy and how it is normally practised.[33] Talmon was not the first to write about working with people who often only attend one session. Indeed, Sigmund Freud wrote about times when he was asked to consult with someone when he was on vacation and was able to help them in one session (e.g., Freud & Breuer, 1895).

Therapists, in general, are very suspicious when it transpires that a client has only come once.[34] They refer to the client as having 'dropped-out' of treatment or having terminated therapy 'prematurely'. However, these somewhat pejorative remarks are decidedly from the therapist's perspective. While not wishing to deny the fact that, in some cases, a person deciding not to return for a second therapy session indicates dissatisfaction with the first session, research and service data show that clients who decide to come once are often satisfied with the help they have received in the first (and only) session and decide not to seek further help. These data are more pronounced when this form of

---

[33] This chapter was originally published as Dryden, W. (2023). What's in a name? What to call therapy when a client may come once. *Inside Out*, 100, 12–14. It appears here in updated form with the publisher's kind permission.

[34] Data from agencies across the world indicate that the most frequent number of sessions clients have is '1'. (e.g., Brown & Jones, 2005; Hoyt & Talmon, 2014). This is formally known as the 'mode'.

therapy delivery is planned and contracted, that is where the therapist and client agree to meet to help the client get what they came for in that one session on the understanding that more help is available to the client on request.

While this way of working with people challenges received therapeutic wisdom such as 'it takes time to forge a good therapeutic relationship which cannot be done in one session',[35] another challenge is posed by what to call this mode of therapy delivery.

In this chapter, I will consider the issues one faces when deciding what to call therapy where the intent is to help the person in one session but where more help is available. I will review the two names currently used, Single-Session Therapy (SST) and One-At-A-Time Therapy (OAATT), and explain my reservations about them. Then, I will explain why I prefer the term ONEplus Therapy.

Single-Session Therapy

Whenever I give a training workshop on single-session therapy, I emphasise that the purpose of SST is for the therapist and client to work together to see if they can help the client meet their stated wants from the session while acknowledging that more help is available to the client if requested. However, people continue to hear that the nature of single-session therapy is that it provides therapy lasting one session only. They sometimes refer to this as 'one-off' therapy. These people then argue that in SST, we restrict help offered to people and only offer them one session when they want more. This is decidedly not the case.

However, the difficulty here is that single-session therapy *can* last for one session only. This occurs when the client states in advance that this is all they want, and the therapist concurs with this. Yet, single-session therapy can *also* refer to the situation mentioned above, where it can be one session but involves additional help. Jeffrey Young (2018) acknowledges the difficulties inherent in the term 'single-session therapy' but

---

[35] See Dryden (2022c) for a discussion of this and other ways in which this mode of therapy delivery challenges mor conventional ways of thinking about therapy.

argues for its retention because it has 'shock' value – it interests and challenges therapists new to this mode of therapy delivery. I understand this viewpoint, but as 'clarity' is one of the central principles of this mode of therapy delivery, there should be, in my opinion, a description of this way of working with people that is clear and accurate. Given the ambiguity surrounding the term 'single-session therapy', my approach is to look for a different, unambiguous descriptive term.

One-At-A-Time Therapy

Michael Hoyt (2011) introduced the term 'one at a time' to refer to SST. Hoyt, Bobele, Slive, Young & Talmon (2018: 5) state that this term describes the situation where 'therapy takes place one contact at a time, and one contact may be all the time that is needed.' However, particularly in university and college counselling services in the United Kingdom, 'One-At-A-Time Therapy' (OAATT) has been used to describe a situation where students can only book one session at a time after which a 'purposeful pause'[36] takes place so that students have an opportunity to get the maximum benefit from the session by implementing what they have learned before they can make another appointment. This practice reflects the situation in other agencies where clients are told that they will be contacted two weeks (for example) after their single session and asked how they are getting on and to see if they require further help.

In OAATT, it is not possible for a client to access any other mode of therapy delivery, such as ongoing therapy, once they have decided they need more help.

In both SST and OAATT, an integral part of the offer is that the 'session' includes the time after the meeting between therapist and client where the client implements what they have learned in the session and decides at that point if they need more help.

---

[36] More formally here, at the end of the session, clients are asked to engage in a process called 'reflect-digest-act-let time pass-decide' where they are encouraged to reflect on their learning from the session, to digest it (meaning to make connections with other relevant areas of their life), to act on their reflections and digested learning and to see what happens before they decide to whether or not to seek more help.

ONEplus Therapy

Given that I have reservations concerning the terms 'single-session therapy' and 'one-at-a-time therapy', what do I suggest instead? I have decided to call the mode of therapy delivery 'ONEplus Therapy' (see Dryden, 2023). I have capitalised the word 'ONE' because it indicates it is a principal objective of this way of working to help the person with what they have come for by the end of the session. The word 'plus' is attached to the word 'ONE' without a space to indicate that more help is available to the client on request and that this is an integral part of the delivery mode. Like SST and OAATT, 'ONEplus therapy' encourages the person to implement their learning from the session before deciding if they need more help. The 'plus' emphasises that the client can access *any* form of therapy delivery offered by the agency or practitioner. If they request a form of help not provided by the above, then, if possible, a suitable external referral is made.

In addition, given the dual nature of this way of working ('let's help you in one session/more help is available), the term 'ONEplus therapy' does not suggest that only one session is offered to the client, which, in the minds of many, is suggested by the term 'single-session therapy'. I hope that the term 'ONEplus Therapy' clarifies the essence of what we try to do in offering this mode of therapy delivery. This is to offer therapy where the therapist and client contract to meet for a session of therapy and work together to help the client to achieve their stated wants from that session on the understanding that further help is available to the client on request after the client has derived maximum benefit from the session by implementing what they learned from it.

9

Single-Session Therapy and the Therapist's Fear of Opening Up a Can of Worms

Many therapists in the single-session therapy community consider that its practice is best informed by a set of beliefs collectively referred to as the 'single-session therapy mindset' (Cannistrà, 2022) or 'single-session thinking' (Hoyt, Young, and Rycroft, 2021).[37] When therapists first encounter SST, they will likely bring to bear what I have called the 'conventional therapy mindset' (Dryden, 2023a) when appraising SST. Many frequently asked questions (FAQs) that therapists pose about SST come from those with this latter mindset (Dryden, 2022). As such, when responding to these questions, it is vital to consider this difference in mindset.

One of the concerns that therapists have about SST is that it opens a 'can of worms'[38] for clients. The phrase 'can of worms' seems to originate from the USA in the 1950s, where anglers would buy sealed metal cans of live worms for bait. When they opened a can, if they did not take care to close it, then the live worms would escape, and the fishermen's attention would shift from catching fish to recapturing the live worms, and chaos would result. According to this scenario, opening a can of worms is not the problem. It is the fisherman's lack of care to close the

---

[37] This chapter was originally published as Dryden, W. (2023). Single-session therapy and the therapist's fear of opening up a can of worms. *Inside Out, 101,* 37–9. It appears here in updated form with the kind permission of the publisher.
[38] In my view, it is disrespectful to liken a client's issues to 'worms'. However, I will use the 'can of worms' analogy here because other therapists use it when expressing their fears about SST.

can before other worms can get out.

By using the 'opening up a can of worms' analogy, the therapist, new to SST, fears that the SST practitioner would do the same as a careless angler: by asking the client to discuss a concern, they would not take care with the result that the client's other problems would spill out and not be contained with the consequence that the client would be harmed.

While I cannot say this would never happen in SST, several factors would reduce the chances of this happening.

Gain the Client's Informed Consent

Single-session therapy, as with other forms of therapy delivery, is based on informed consent. Here, the client consents to work with the therapist on the understanding that the latter will help them achieve what they want by the end of the session with the knowledge that further help is available to them if needed. When the client knows and consents to the parameters of SST, this has a containing effect on them.

Orient the Client to Their Session Goal

Thus, the client is coming to therapy with the idea that they and the therapist will work together with their goal firmly in mind. If the client's goal cannot be achieved, the therapist will be honest in telling them what they can and cannot help them with, leading to the setting of an achievable goal. The main point here is that the client's achievable goal provides the focus for the work. Thus, the goal-oriented focus of the session provides additional therapeutic containment so that only one 'worm', i.e., client issue, is let out of the 'can'.

Agree on a Therapeutic Focus

Whether the therapeutic focus is on the client's issue or goal, the purpose of a focus is to provide an opportunity for the client to give their attention to one issue. If they have only one issue, then the 'can of worms' phenomenon is irrelevant. Here, the client's 'can' contains only one 'worm'. If the client has other issues, the focus is on one agreed issue. This focus helps the therapist and client deal with the issue in the knowledge that while the client may have other issues (other 'worms' in the 'can'), the therapeutic focus helps the client deal with one issue ('worm') at a time. In doing so, the therapist keeps the lid on the 'can' so that the other issues ('worms') can be dealt with, perhaps later.

Seek the Client's Permission to Be Interrupted

One of the critical skills employed by the SST therapist is interrupting the client when the client departs from the agreed focus. As I have mentioned elsewhere (Dryden, 2023a), the best way for the therapist to do this is to give the client a rationale for interrupting them, gain their permission to do so, and agree on the best way for them to do it, if necessary. As the primary purpose of interrupting the client is to maintain the agreed focus, doing so ensures that the issue remains the object of discussion. It helps the client to put back into the 'can' other 'worms' (issues) that may be struggling to escape.

Check In with the Client

It is also common practice for the SST therapist to check with the client periodically that the client is discussing what they want to discuss. Using our analogy, is the 'worm' the one the angler (client) wishes to use as bait (concentrate on)? If so, then the two proceed with the agreed focus. If not, and there is time, the focus is shifted to a more relevant issue. If checking in is not done, there is the risk that the agreed therapeutic focus is incorrect, and the more relevant issue ('worm') will weigh on the client's now divided mind (another 'worm' will seek to escape from the 'can'). Thus, checking in allows the client to talk about what they want to discuss, reducing the situation where other issues ('worms') compete for attention (escape from the 'can').

Manage the Client's Distress

The fear of 'opening up a can of worms' is related to the concern that the client may become so distressed that the therapist would not be able to help them contain it, so they leave the session in a very distressed state and experience harm as a result. If this happens, the therapist has failed to follow the abovementioned guidelines. The skilled SST therapist can facilitate the client's emotional engagement with their chosen issue while helping them to contain their emotions. A further appointment is strongly indicated if the client is flooded with emotions which cannot be contained.

Offer More Help If Needed

One of the problems with the term 'single-session therapy' is that no matter how many times it is stressed to therapists new to SST that it does not mean a one-off session and that more help is available to the client if needed, the term is often taken literally to mean therapy that lasts for a single session. This is why I have described my work in this area under the term 'ONEplus Therapy' (Dryden, 2023b). The fact that more help is available to the client and that both they and their therapist know this at the outset is in itself containing for the client who has several issues to deal with. Knowing this, the client does not feel pressured to mention all of their issues in one session sues and risk the escape of more 'worms' than they can process.

In conclusion, the skilled single-session therapist is aware of the risk of the session 'opening up a can of worms' for the client and guards against this happening by (a) ensuring that the client understands and consents to the session, which is designed to help them achieve what they have come for; (b) by being focused on the client's nominated problem and goal for the session; (c) maintaining this focus by interrupting the client and checking in with them to ensure that as the session unfolds they are still discussing what they want to discuss; and (d) ensuring that the client knows both at the outset and the end of the session that they can have more help if needed. However, as discussed in Chapter 8, this help is usually offered after the client has had the opportunity to apply what they learned in the session to their everyday life. Only then, can they make an informed decision about seeking more help.

10

Dealing with Risk and Minimising Harm in Single-Session Therapy

Introduction

Many practitioners new to single-session therapy have concerns that clients who are at risk will be poorly served in SST and that clients, in general, may be harmed by this mode of therapy delivery. Such concerns are based on a failure to understand SST and how it is practised. In this chapter, I will consider both issues: how SST therapists deal with risk and how they strive to minimise client harm. First, let me offer a definition of single-session therapy that will clarify how I am using the term in this chapter.

> 'Single-Session Therapy is an intentional endeavour where therapist and client consent to work with one another to help the client to achieve their stated wants from the session on the understanding that further help is available to the client on request after the client has had an opportunity to apply what they have learned from the session to their life and decide if such help is necessary.'

Dealing with Risk in SST

One of the most frequent questions I get asked whenever I give a presentation or workshop on single-session therapy (SST) is, 'How is risk managed in SST?' (Dryden, 2022). My response is that a therapist manages risk in SST like in any other form of therapy delivery. In some therapy agencies, the therapist is mandated to do a risk assessment of every new client seeking help. If a risk is identified, the therapist deals with it in the same way as is typical in that agency. If a risk is not identified, the therapist and the client proceed with the single session.

In other agencies, therapists are encouraged to explore risk with their clients only when they are concerned with something, a client has said during the single session. When this happens, the therapist is transparent with the client that they are concerned about something that the client has said, and as such, they will explore risk carefully with the client. Suppose a therapist is mandated to do a risk assessment by their employing agency at the beginning of the session. In that case, the question arises, what type of routine risk assessment can be done which satisfies the agency but does not intrude into the SST process? This is how such a risk assessment can be done:

Therapist: Before we start, may I ask you a few questions that I have to ask all my clients concerning risk?

Client: OK.

Therapist: Concerning risk, do you consider that you are at risk to yourself at the moment or shortly?

Client: No, I don't.

Therapist: Any thoughts of taking your own life or harming yourself?

Client: None at all.

Therapist: Do you consider that you pose a risk to the life or well-being of another person or other people now or shortly?

Client: No.

Therapist: Any thoughts of harming another person?

Client: No.

Therapist: Finally, do you consider that you pose a risk to the life or well-being of a pet or other animal?

Client: No.

Therapist: Any thoughts of harming an animal?

Client: None.

Therapist: Finally, would you be honest with me if you did pose a risk to yourself, another person or animal?

Client: Yes, I would.

If the client answers any of the therapist's questions affirmatively, the therapist will explore risk with the client in a more detailed manner. However, they can get on with the single-session work if this is not the case. Exploring risk in an SST context with every client is neither warranted nor a fair use of valuable therapeutic time.

I have said that a therapist would deal with risk like in every other therapy delivery mode. Given that the client's wait for a session is minimal in SST by appointment and non-existent in SST by 'open-access, enter-now'[39] if the client is at risk, the therapist quickly discovers this and can promptly deal with it. Doing so renders the client safer than they would be if they received help at the point of availability.

If the therapist does a structured risk assessment at the beginning of the session and the client does not reveal risk, this, of course mean that the client is not at risk. As the session unfolds it may transpire that the client mentions something that the therapist is concerned about and in this case the therapist needs to initiate a conversation about risk even though it may be uncomfortable for them to do so.

---

[39] 'Open-access, enter-now' services is the name now given to walk-in therapy. The latter term is deemed to exclude those who cannot walk.

Minimising Client Harm in SST

Client harm is best conceptualised as client-experienced harm. This occurs when a client believes they have been harmed due to having treatment from a therapist (Parry, Crawford & Duggan, 2016). There has been little research on this topic in the field of psychotherapy, in general, let alone in the specific area of single-session therapy. Therefore, I will extrapolate from the research done in the general field of psychotherapy to the specific area of SST. In doing so, I say that clients can be harmed in SST in the sense that clients can be harmed in any type of therapy, both in long-term work and in the ultra-brief work that is SST. In stating that clients can be harmed in SST, I will consider what SST practitioners can do to minimise client harm.

In reporting on several risk factors for harm, Hardy, Bishop-Edwards, Chambers, Connell, Dent-Brown, Kothari, O'Hara & Parry (2019: 403) argue that such harm can be minimised by clients being given 'clear information, choice, involvement in decision-making, explicit contracting and clarity about sessions and progress'.

The following factors can limit the possibility of harm befalling clients in SST.

Giving the Client Clear Information about the Realistic Nature of SST

Clients should be given explicit information about SST and what can and can't be achieved in this mode of therapy delivery. Harm may befall a client if they enter SST with high and unrealistic expectations, which are not met by the end of the session. Consequently, the therapist needs to have a transparent discussion with the client on this point, correcting any misconceptions the person may have about what can be achieved from SST. I usually say that SST sparks the beginning of a change process rather than brings it to a conclusion.

Promoting Choice and Decision-Making

When SST sits alongside other therapy delivery modes, then clients must be given information about each mode so that they can select the one that they consider best suited to their needs.

This information should include the time they must wait to access each service. In my view, harm is more likely to be experienced by a client who has been assigned a therapy delivery mode that they have had no say in selecting than by a client who has selected SST because they have decided it best suits their current needs.

Explicit Contracting

Before contracting with the client, the therapist must clarify that SST involves them working with the client to achieve the latter's stated wants from the session and that more help is available if required. The client must know that appropriate help is available if they need further help after the single session. If it is unavailable when the client has been led to believe it will be, there is the potential for harm. Thus, the therapist should be very clear with the client about which services will be and will not be accessible to the client after the session.

Curran, Parry, Hardy, Darling, Mason & Chambers (2019) analysed qualitative research studies on clients' harmful therapy experiences. What SST practitioners can learn from this research that is relevant to harm reduction in SST is as follows.

Forming a Good Therapeutic Alliance

An excellent therapeutic alliance in SST is formed when the therapist shows the client respect by taking their stated wants (session goals) seriously and helping them achieve them or take a significant step towards doing so. It is also facilitated when the therapist is transparent about what they can and cannot do in SST and demonstrates an empathic understanding of the client's nominated concern. An excellent therapeutic alliance predicts a good SST outcome, preventing client harm (Simon, Imel, Ludman & Steinfeld, 2012).

Providing a Flexible Therapeutic Response

Curran et al. (2019) found that clients who considered their therapist inflexible were more likely to experience harm than those who found their therapist to be flexible and tailored to their needs. Given that SST is client-led rather than therapist-led is, in my view, a protective factor against client harm in this mode of therapy delivery.

Containing Client Distress

Because SST can be regarded as ultra-brief therapy, the prospect of a client experiencing harm due to the therapist being over-involved with their client is lessened. Therefore there is less chance of there being boundary violations by the therapist in SST than in longer-term therapy unless they know the client in another context. A client is at risk of harm in SST if they open up in the session and do not get a containing response from their therapist. Therapist containment of client distress in the session is an important protective factor against client harm, mainly if the client is offered appropriate follow-up help at the end of the session.[40] If this is not done, then it increases the chances of client harm. In my experience, this is more likely to happen when the therapist has been inadequately trained and supervised in SST. I will discuss the importance of SST training and supervision at the end of this piece.

The Unfortunate Case of Critical Incident Stress Debriefing

In a review of psychological treatments that cause harm, Lilienfeld (2007) lists one single-session treatment, known as 'critical incident stress debriefing' (CISD), that has been shown to have long-term harmful effects on people exposed to stressors. However, there are a lot of elements of CISD that are absent in SST. Thus, it is a group session lasting three to four hours and people exposed to a common extreme stressor are expected, and some would say, coerced, to attend the session. As Lilienfeld (2007: 59) notes, 'CISD therapists (a) strongly encourage group members to discuss and "process" their negative emotions, (b)

---

[40] While the offer in SST is that further help is available after the client has had the opportunity to apply what they learned in the session to their life and then decide if they want to seek such help, flexibility in SST means that there are times when it is advisable to offer the client further help at the end of the session. Not doing so, when the client is highly distressed increases the chances of harm in SST.

delineate the PTSD symptoms that group members are likely to experience, and (c) discourage members from discontinuing participation once the session has begun. Thus, CISD is not client-focused. The therapist sets the agenda, pressurises people to do things they may not be ready to do, details experiences that clients may not have had, and compels them to remain in a situation they wish to leave. These factors are the antithesis of collaborative and client-led SST practice. It would be a shame if CISD were cited as evidence that SST should not be used in agencies because of its harmful effects. This iatrogenic treatment shares only one feature with SST – it lasts for a lengthy and, I would say.'

The Importance of Training and Supervision

In this chapter, I have made two points. First, single-session therapy can be used to help clients at risk. Second, while all modes of therapy delivery have the potential to cause clients harm, there are six ways in which such harm can be minimised in SST. Single-session therapists need to be adequately trained and supervised to respond to risk and minimise client harm. I have outlined my views of what such training and supervision should look like in Dryden (2023). My concern is that therapists are practising SST without sufficient training to do the work and are being supervised by people who have neither been trained in SST nor have done the work themselves. If this situation is addressed, then the concerns that SST does not respond to client risk and leads to client harm will be addressed.

11

The Single-Session Therapy Mindset and How It Informs Practice

Preamble

As I mentioned in the Preface, the more experience I have gained as a single-session therapist, trainer and supervisor, the clearer I have become concerning the central role that bringing a single-session therapy mindset to the practice of SST holds. Consequently, no collection of my work on SST can go forward to publication without a chapter devoted to this vital topic.[41]

Introduction

In my view, the most crucial ingredient in helping a therapist to become a skilled single-session practitioner is the mindset they bring to this work. Cannistrà (2022: 1) states that a mindset is 'the therapist's series of beliefs which influence the actions and decisions taken in the course of their work.' In this chapter, I will outline the main elements of the single-session therapy mindset, which therapists are advised to bring to their implementation of this mode of therapy delivery. I will also show how this mindset informs the practice of single-session therapy. Compare this mindset with what I call the 'conventional therapy mindset' that underpins the delivery of traditional therapy, where the client and therapist are expected to spend more than one session together, often a lot more (see Appendix 2).

---

[41] This chapter is an updated version of material published in Dryden, W. (2023). *ONEplus Therapy: Help at the Point of Need.* Onlinevents Publications (pp. 28–46). It appears here with the kind permission of the publisher.

One Session or More: Be Open to Both Possibilities

As I have emphasised, the defining feature of single-session therapy is that the therapist and the client meet to help the person take away from the session what they have come for on the understanding that more help is available to the person on request. The therapist is advised to keep both ideas in mind as they approach the session and be open to both possibilities, prioritising neither.

It Is Possible to Conduct a Session without Prior Knowledge of the Person

As I will discuss in the following chapter, some single-session therapists send their clients a pre-session form to complete, primarily to help their clients prepare for their session to get the most from it. These clients are invited to share their completed forms with their therapists so that the latter can also prepare for the session. Clients are informed that the completion and/or return of the form is not mandatory, just recommended. Some clients choose not to complete the form; others do it but decide not to return it. This does not mean that they can't have the session. It means that their therapist will see the client without any prior information about them. This is acceptable in single-session therapy, where seeing clients without prior knowledge about them is common. For example, this frequently happens in open-access, enter-now therapy,[42] and all the time when I do live demonstrations of single-session therapy for professionals (Dryden, 2021a).

Indeed, sometimes, having prior knowledge about a client can pose a problem. Thus, a client may return their pre-session preparation form stating that they want to address an anger issue, but on the day, they want to discuss an anxiety problem. If the therapist expects to deal with the former, it may throw them when the latter is presented. So, the therapist should keep in mind any

---

[42] This was previously known as walk-in therapy. However, the term 'walk-in' was deemed to be problematic for those who are unable to walk. Thus, the term open-access, enter-now therapy is currently considered more inclusive and this preferred.

information they may have about a client but be prepared to let it go in favour of the client's stated wants from the session.

While some therapists who offer more ongoing forms of therapy require a referral letter or insist upon an assessment session before deciding on whether to offer therapy to a client, not having such knowledge about a client is not a barrier to seeing someone in single-session therapy.

Start Therapy from the First Moment

It is vital to remember that the purpose of the first (and perhaps only) single-session therapy session that a therapist may have with the client is to provide them with the form of help they seek, not the form of help the therapist thinks they need. This is reflected in how a therapist might begin the session, which I discussed in Chapter 5. Volunteers at the Samaritans[43] answer calls to their telephone line with 'Hello, this is the Samaritans. How can I help you?', and not with 'Hello, this is the Samaritans. How can I assess you?' Thus, a single-session therapist should remember that they are there to provide straightaway the therapeutic help requested by the client unless there is a good reason not to do so. Consequently, they are advised to cut to the therapeutic chase at the outset and ask one of several questions designed to initiate therapy immediately (see Chapter 5).

View the Session as a Whole, Complete in Itself

The single-session therapist approaches the session as if it is the only time that they will meet the person (while allowing for the possibility that it might not be) and that this will be a complete session that lasts for a duration determined by both.[44] This being

---

[43] The Samaritans is a registered charity aimed at providing emotional support to anyone in emotional distress, struggling to cope or at risk of suicide throughout the United Kingdom and the Republic of Ireland, often through its telephone helpline.

[44] Sessions in single-session therapy can be of varying lengths. In my practice, I offer a client a session of *up to* 50 minutes. I do this because if we finish earlier, then it's better to end the session when the work is done than when the clock determines the session's end. I used to work for an online service which offered clients 30-minute video therapy sessions. While clients in this service

said, there *may* be pre-session contact through the completion and return of a form, and there *may* be post-session contact when the client has requested further help. Also, the session has its process with a beginning, a middle and an end.

Potentially, Anyone Can Be Helped in a Single Session

One of the questions people frequently ask me during the training workshops I offer in single-session therapy is which clients can and cannot be helped in SST. My view is that a single-session therapist can help *anyone*, but they will not be able to help *everyone*. Given that the therapist will only be able to know if the client found the session helpful at the end of the session, they should not decline to help someone until it becomes clear that they can't. This is a significant principle behind open-access, enter-now therapy and is one of the ways in which this mode of therapy delivery influences single-session therapy by appointment. Consequently, the therapist does not need to engage in any pre-therapy exploration with the client concerning their suitability or non-suitability for single-session therapy. The critical issue is whether the client understands single-session therapy and wants to access it. If the answer to the first question is 'no', then the therapist should help them to understand it. If the answer to the second question is 'no', the therapist should not don't proceed with single-session therapy but discover what form of help the client wishes to access and offer it to them if they or the agency in which they work can do so.

Focus on the Person, Not the Disorder

Following on from the above, it is vital that the therapist focuses on their client as a unique individual and not as a representative of a category indicating a mental health disorder. Thus, when I am asked a question such as, 'Can someone with 'x' disorder be helped in single-session therapy?' my response is, 'What is the person's name, and what do they want to achieve from the session?'

---

could have from five to eight sessions, most attended one session (see Chapter 12).

This focus on the person and not the disorder is demonstrated in the following example. A person diagnosed with psychosis sought help from a walk-in clinic in a state of anxiety. What had been happening was that the client's landlord had found him agitated, talking to himself and was concerned that the client posed a risk to others in his building. He, thus, threatened the client with eviction. In the session, the therapist first responded by suggesting that the client might wish to review his medication with his psychiatrist, which he agreed to do. Then, as the client stated that his goal was to keep his accommodation, the therapist suggested that they role-played how the client could talk to his landlord to allay the latter's fears about the client posing a risk to the household. They did this, and the client implemented this solution with his landlord and successfully retained his accommodation. He was still diagnosed as psychotic, but he was psychotic and safe in his living quarters rather than psychotic and vulnerable living on the streets.

Again, the answer to the question, can this person with a disorder benefit from single-session therapy, is that if they understand it and want to access it, offer it to them and see if they benefit from it by the end of the session.

The Client–Therapist Relationship Can Be Established Rapidly

Another frequently asked question about single-session therapy concerns the questioner's doubts about whether a productive relationship can be established with the client in this mode of service delivery. My response is a resounding, 'Yes, it can'. Taking Bordin's (1979) tripartite view of the working alliance and my elaboration of it (Dryden, 2011), the following explains why I am clear in my answer. A good working alliance between client and therapist is demonstrated by the pair having a good bond, shared views about therapy, an agreement on the client's goals and an agreed pathway towards these goals. In single-session therapy, a good working alliance is evidenced by the following.

Shared Views

The therapist and client agree to meet to help the client take away from the session their stated wants) and on the understanding that more help is available to the client on request after they have the chance to implement what they learned from the session.

Agreement on the Client's Goal

The therapist and client agree that the focus of the session will be on the client's goals.

Effective Bond

The effective SST therapist shows respect for the client (a) by demonstrating a keenness to help the person in the way that they wish to be helped, (b) by expressing their understanding of how the client sees things, and (c) by being transparent. This means that the therapist makes explicit:

- What single-session therapy is and what it isn't;
- What they can do and can't do in single-session therapy;
- At the appropriate time, what further help is available, and how long the client will have to wait for it;
- The reasons for their major interventions;
- Their answers to any questions their client has about single-session therapy.

Agreed Pathway towards the Client's Goals (Agreed Tasks)

Once the therapist has established the client's preferred way of being helped, they adjust their interventions to match the client's preferences in this respect. Most of the time, this will be the client wanting a solution to their problem. In this case, the therapist's task is to help them discover a solution they can integrate into their life and implement after the session.

Simon, Imel, Ludman & Steinfeld (2012) found that those clients who benefited from a single session of therapy reported forming a better working alliance with their therapists along the above lines than clients who did not benefit from it.

Single-Session Therapy Is Client Led

One of the most critical aspects of the single-session therapy mindset is that the client determines what happens in SSST. This is demonstrated by the client taking the lead:

- By indicating the help that they are seeking from the therapist;
- By setting the goal for the session;
- By playing an active role in creating a focus for the session;
- By selecting what they regard as the best solution to their nominated problem.

The single-session therapist will keep these points in mind in working with the client in this form of therapy delivery and make interventions to encourage them to take the lead.

The Client Decides How Much Therapy They Want

In many therapy agencies, the agency decides how much therapy a client will get. In such cases, the client is offered a block of sessions – often six – which may be reviewed again, mainly at the behest of the therapist. In single-session therapy, the client decides how much therapy they want, often opting for a single session because they have received the help they had been looking for from that session. Unless the therapist has internalised this feature of the SST mindset, they will tend to think during the session that the client needs more therapy because they can discern beneath the surface of the client's narrative that they have more problems that require therapeutic attention. When reviewing the client's future options concerning further help once the client has had the chance to implement their takeaways from the session, if the therapist thinks the client needs more help, they will express this opinion in some way that may influence the client to select the additional help option.

When the therapist adopts the principle that the client decides how much therapy they want, they will present three options after the client has had an opportunity to put into practice what they have learned from the session, if the issue of further help comes up for review.

'We have three ways forward, and each option is equally fine. First, you can decide that you have gotten the help you have come for and don't need further help. Second, you can decide that you need further help, and we can discuss what kind of help that might be and book an appointment now. Finally, you can decide that you would like more time to implement your takeaways from the session, see how things go and contact us again if you would like more help. As I have said, each option is equally OK. Which option is the best one for you?'

Identify and Meet the Client's Preference for Being Helped

While the most frequently requested form of help that clients seek from single-session therapy is with a specific emotional or behavioural problem with which they feel stuck (see Chapter 12), this is by no means the only type of help a therapist can offer in SST. When the therapist asks their client what kind of help they are looking for from them, the client may be unable to respond with clarity. Thus, they may need clarification about what type of help they seek, in this case, the therapist can outline the various helping options on offer. Thus, the therapist can help the client to:

- Develop a greater understanding of their nominated issue;
- Talk about the issue while the therapist listens;
- Express their feelings about the issue;
- Solve an emotional or behavioural problem with which they feel stuck;
- Make a decision;
- Resolve a dilemma;
- Talk about whatever they want to talk about in their own way.

In addition, they may wish the therapist to:

- Give them a professional opinion on something; or
- Signpost them to appropriate services.

Having outlined these helping options, the therapist can then ask them to select the one that most closely matches the help they seek. Such matching is vital. As Norcross & Cooper (2021) note, when the therapist helps the client in the way they wish to be helped, rather than in the way the therapist thinks the client needs, then a better therapeutic outcome is more likely.

Keep in Mind the Importance of Negotiating an End-of-Session Goal with the Client

When the client is asked about their goals in conventional therapy, it concerns what they want to achieve by the end of therapy. In single-session therapy, the therapist asks the client what they want to accomplish by the end of the session. This emphasis on a session goal helps to focus both the therapist and the client and provides a direction for the session.

I distinguish between a session goal and a problem-related goal. The latter is what the client wants to achieve in relation to their nominated problem. In this context, a session goal can be finding a solution to the nominated problem that the client can implement to work towards achieving their problem-related goal. This is shown diagrammatically thus:

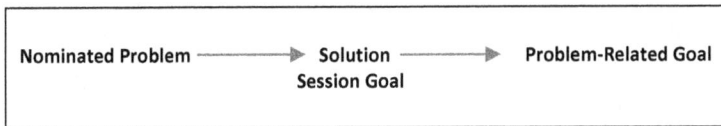

```
Nominated Problem ──────▶ Solution ──────▶ Problem-Related Goal
                         Session Goal
```

Keep in Mind the Importance of Co-Creating a Therapeutic Focus and Maintaining It Once It Has Been Created

Aside from the situation where the client wants to have the opportunity to talk about whatever they want to talk about in whichever way they want to talk about it, single-session therapy is best done with focus. This focus needs to be co-created with the client, related to the session goal, and relevant to the client's nominated problem.

Once the focus has been decided upon, it is important to maintain it. It is the therapist's responsibility as a single-session therapist to do this. The therapist may need to interrupt the client to help them return to the focus if they have moved away from it. The best way that a therapist can do this is to give the client a rationale for interrupting them, gain their assent for them to do this, and agree on how they will interrupt the client. It is also helpful for the therapist to check in periodically with the client to determine that they are still discussing what they want to talk about with the therapist.

Unless the Client's Preference is to the Contrary, a Single-Session Therapy Session Requires a Structure

As I pointed out earlier, the therapist can provide different types of help in single-session therapy. That being said, the most common form of help clients seek from this mode of therapy delivery is emotional/behavioural problem-solving. Providing such help means adhering to a particular structure for the session. This is as follows.

The Beginning Phase

Here, the therapist and client agree on the purpose of their meeting and make a contract for the session. Then, the therapist and client agree on a goal for the session and co-create a focus. The therapist can then assess the client's nominated problem.[45]

The Middle Phase

In the middle phase of single-session therapy, the emphasis is on helping the client to find a solution to their nominated problem. Here, several relevant factors come into play, including the client's previous helpful attempts to address the problem, the opposite of the factors that maintain their problem, the client's internal strengths and external resources, the client's view of

---

[45] Single-session therapists who practise solution focused therapy may omit this step.

what may help and the therapist's view of what may help. Different solutions may be discussed until one is settled on, and at this point, the therapist can help the client to rehearse the solution, if feasible. The therapist can then help the client to think of ways to implement this solution, and finally, the therapist works with the client to identify and address obstacles to such implementation.

The End Phase

At this point, the therapist is ready to bring the session to a close. First, the therapist can ask the client to summarise what has been covered in the session. In particular, the therapist should encourage the client to identify their takeaways from the session and review how they will implement these in their life. If possible, the therapist encourages the client o see how they can generalise their learning to other problems that they may have. Before the end, the therapist should encourage the client to ask any last-minute questions, which they will answer and to tell them anything that wraps things up for them. The therapist should stress here that this is not an opportunity for the client to discuss a new problem. The therapist should end the session by encouraging the client to implement what they have learned in the session, reminding them that they can get more help in the future if they wish.

Complex Problems Do Not Always Require Complex Solutions

The point is often made by therapists adhering to a conventional therapy mindset that single-session therapy is not suitable to help people with complex problems because they need far more time than a single session to be helped. My response is, 'It depends'. First, a therapist may be able to help a person with a complex problem because just because a problem is complex, it does not follow that the solution has to be complex. Second, a person with a complex problem may seek help for another problem that is not complex. Third, the person with a complex problem may benefit from taking a 'one step at a time' approach to this problem. Finally, the therapist should remember that single-session therapy does not preclude the person from having ongoing therapy for their complex problem should this option be available to them, and they choose to use it.

Focus on What the Person Has Done Before Concerning the Problem

Usually, the client will have made several attempts to help themself with their problem. As they still have the problem, the therapist might be excused for thinking that nothing that the client has done in the past to help themself has any merit. However, this is not necessarily the case. It is worthwhile for the therapist to consider the importance of reviewing with the client what they did in the past to address the issue and what was in any way helpful to them and what was not beneficial.

The therapist can also think of doing this with how they have addressed past similar and non-similar problems. This may help the therapist to identify strategies that the client has successfully used in the past that they may be able to transfer to the work that the two of them are doing together on their nominated problem.

One question that can be particularly helpful is, 'Think of a personal problem that you solved in the past that, as you look back, you are particularly proud of. What did you do that you were most proud of?' This question can be useful in two ways. First, it can give the therapist and their client *specific* information about what the client can use to address their nominated problem in single-session therapy. Second, it may give the client a *general* sense of their ability to be a good problem-solver that they may use to address their current issue.

Focus on the Client's Internal Strengths and External Resources

A single-session therapist needs to keep in mind that if they are to help the person take away what they have come for from the session, they will need to identify and make use of both the client's internal strengths and external resources. When the therapist does this, they encourage the client to address their problem under favourable conditions.

Failing to do this is like trying to repair a building with shaky foundations. First, strengthen the foundations and then repair the building. Here are some ways that the therapist can elicit such information in the course of single-session therapy.

Internal Strengths

In the course of the client telling the therapist about their nominated problem and how they have tried to address it in the past, the therapist will be able to hear the client express strengths that they have. In their responses, the therapist can refer to these as strengths that the client may use in addressing the problem and discuss how they might do so. The therapist can also ask the client for their strengths more directly (see Chapter 9 in Dryden, 2023).

External Resources

Again, when the client tells the therapist about their nominated problem and how they have tried to address it, they may refer to other people. The therapist should determine which people have been helpful to the client and how they have been of help. The therapist should encourage the client to consider recruiting these people as they work towards addressing their nominated problem after the session has finished (see Chapter 9 in Dryden, 2023). In making suggestions to the client about potentially useful organisations and other external resources, it is vital that the therapist does not overwhelm them with too much information. One or two suggestions will usually suffice.

Keep in Mind that Different Methods Can Be Used with Different Clients

Given that single-session therapy clients differ from one another and will want different things from the session, it is vital for the therapist to bear this in mind when considering what help to offer them. Does it make sense for the therapist to approach the session thinking that no matter what clients bring, they will use the same methods with each of them? Of course not. So, the therapist needs to remember that they will need to use different methods with different clients.

The therapist should check with clients concerning the methods they consider may be helpful to them. In this respect, for example, I have found it useful to ask clients if they find imagery methods helpful. If so, I will make use of such methods during the session.

Adopt a Solution-Focused Orientation, if Relevant

As I made clear above, a single-session therapist needs to be prepared to approach the session remembering that different clients will be seeking different forms of help from them, and they should be prepared to offer them the help that they seek unless there is a good reason not to do so. The therapist should also note that most people seeking single-session therapy will do so because they seek help with a specific emotional/behavioural problem with which they have become stuck (see Chapter 12). When this is the case, the therapist needs to remember that they need to help the client find a solution to their nominated problem. In particular, the therapist should bear in mind that a solution addresses the nominated problem and allows the person to achieve their problem-related goal. A solution can involve the client in the following:

- Developing a new way of thinking;
- Changing a relevant attitude;
- Developing a new constructive way of acting (e.g. being assertive);
- Altering some aspect(s) of the environment;
- Developing a new habit to promote their mental well-being (e.g. practising mindfulness regularly);
- Developing a new habit to promote their physical well-being (e.g. taking regular exercise).

In addition, a solution may involve some combination of the above factors.

When developing a solution with the person, it is vital that the therapist and client draw from the following:

- Helpful aspects of the client's previous attempts to solve the problem;
- Helpful aspects of the client's attempts to solve other problems, related and unrelated to the nominated problem;
- Constructive alternatives to problem-maintaining factors;
- The client's relevant strengths;
- Relevant aspects of the external resources available to the client;
- The solution that the client's relevant role model would use;
- The client's views on what would constitute a good solution;
- The therapist's views on what would constitute a good solution.

It is important that the therapist remembers that they and their client should select from the above list and only attempt to include some, not all, factors. It is also vital that the therapist and client both consider that the client is most likely to use a solution regularly that they can integrate into their life. For example, if practising mindfulness is deemed a good solution, the therapist should enquire where and when the client can best carry out this practice.

Keep in Mind the Value of Promoting In-Session Practice

In the same way, that a person would probably not drive a car without taking it out for a test drive, the client needs to rehearse (or 'test drive') a solution before committing to it. Such rehearsal encourages the client to discover what it feels like to use the solution and to judge its effectiveness.

When suggesting in-session rehearsal of solutions, the therapist can draw on the following:

- Imagery methods;
- Role-play;

228 Seizing Moments and Being Useful

- Two-chair dialogue;
- Parts work methods.

The outcome of this rehearsal may be that the client:

- Accepts the solution;
- Makes changes to the solution;
- Rejects the solution.

In the latter case, you need to help your client to seek a different solution, and when found, the client would rehearse this as above. This process would continue until the client has settled upon a solution.

Think about Helping the Client to Plan for Action

A solution is only helpful if implemented; this is an essential point for the therapist to keep in mind while conducting an SST session. Also, the therapist needs to keep in mind the factors that will encourage their client to implement their action plan. These are the client:

- Can integrate the plan into their life;
- Is clear on when to implement the plan, where to implement it and how frequently;
- Keeps in mind the reason for implementing the plan;
- Can identify and deal with any obstacles to them implementing the plan.

Small May Be Beautiful

There is a phenomenon known as quantum change where a sudden, dramatic, and enduring change occurs that affects a broad range of emotions, cognitions and behaviour (Miller & C' de Baca, 2001). While this can happen in single-session therapy, it rarely does. What is more common in this mode of service delivery is that the client makes a small but significant step away from their problem towards their problem-related goal or begins to free themself from a stuck pattern. In the same way that a gardener learns to identify and nurture the early shoots of a recently planted seed, both the therapist and their client should learn to see that such small steps towards growth in the client are, indeed, beautiful and should be encouraged.

Keep in Mind the Importance of Inviting the Client to Summarise the Session

As the therapist approaches the end of the session, they should think about how their client can consolidate what they have learned from the session. One way to do this is for the therapist to consider asking the client to summarise the session. This helps the client stay active in the session and allows them to think about what has stood out for *them* from the session. If the therapist summarises the session for the client, they show the client what has stood out for *the therapist* and this renders the client passive at the very point that they need to be active. The therapist may add to the client's summary, but they should let it still be the client's summary.

Focus on the Client's Takeaway(s)

What the client has learned from the session is important, but if they do not take their learning away and apply it, they haven't gotten the most from the session. Asking what the client will take away from the session and their plans to implement it is a vital part of the process. In doing this, the therapist should remind them of the work that the two of them may have already done on action planning. If the therapist has not done this work, now is the time for them to do it. In single-session therapy, less is more, so it is vital that the therapist does not press the client to take away more than one or two significant learning points that, if implemented, would make a meaningful difference in their life.

Keep in Mind Opportunities to Encourage Generalisation Whenever Possible

When the client has nominated a problem for which they are seeking help, the therapist's prime responsibility in SST is to help them develop a solution to this problem so that they can practice it which will help them to achieve their problem-related goal. Once the therapist has done that and if there is time, it is useful for them to consider the idea that it is helpful to ask the client to determine how they may generalise this solution to other relevant situations and problem areas. It is vital that the therapist thinks about how to build this into the fabric of the session since most clients will not spontaneously generalise their learning as a matter of course. They need help to do so.

Results Are Mainly Achieved Outside the Session

As discussed above, while what happens in the session between the therapist and their client is important in laying the foundations for change, what happens outside the session subsequently is more critical in determining what the client ultimately achieves from single-session therapy. It is important that the therapist bears this in mind as they work with their client.

Help the Client Be Clear about Accessing Further Help if Required

The therapist will need to be clear about the client's options for accessing further help. It is now generally accepted that further help should *not* be offered to the client at the end of the session because the outcome of the client's implementation of what they learned from the session is not known at that point.[46] As such, the therapist should encourage the client to reflect on the session, digest their learning, act on it, let time pass, and then decide if they need more help. At that point, the therapist and client can discuss the client's options.[47]

End the Session Well so that the Client Leaves the Session with Their Morale Restored

In viewing the session as a whole (see above), it is vital to end the session well so that the client can leave with a sense of hope, having had their morale restored. The therapist will want the

---

[46] Unless not doing so puts the client at risk.
[47] See the section above entitled 'The Client Decides How Much Therapy They Want'.

client to leave with all their questions answered and to have had the opportunity to tell them everything they wanted.

Take Nothing for Granted

Finally, the single-session therapist treats their inferences about what the client is capable of and the potency of the external resources available to them as hypotheses to be confirmed or disconfirmed. Holding to this principle means that the therapist takes nothing for granted and will respond to the session's events.

In the final chapter of this collection. I will discuss how I implemented some features of the single-session therapy mindset discussed here in my work for an online health service that offered 30-minute online therapy sessions to their clients.

12

Bringing a Single-Session Mindset to Counselling in an Online Health Service in the UK

Abstract

This chapter outlines the counselling work that I did in the period March 2022–April 2023 for a UK online health service.[48] This work can be described as single-session by default rather than by design, as the modal number of my sessions was '1'. During this time, the service was advertised as providing individuals with between six and eight thirty-minute counselling sessions annually. I show how I brought a single-session mindset to this work and detail my experiences. This chapter is based on my experiences alone, and while there were more than 70 counsellors who worked in a self-employed capacity for the organisation, when I was there, I knew very little about how they worked. I describe my work with one of my clients, present another client's account of their session with me and discuss some helpful and unhelpful aspects of working within the organisation.

The Context

'Scimitar Health' (a pseudonym) is a UK online health service offering online consultations to people with private health

---

[48] This chapter was first published as Dryden, W. (2025). Bringing a single-session mindset to counselling in an online health service in the UK. In Cannistra, F., & Hoyt, M.F. (eds), *Single Session Therapies: Why and How One-At-A-Time Mindsets are Effective.* Routledge. This updated version appears here with the kind permission of the publisher.

insurance with specific companies. These companies contract with 'Scimitar Health' – through the insurance companies – to provide consultations that can be had with GPs, physiotherapists, nutritionists, mental health counsellors, and life coaches. The consultations were accessed and booked through a mobile phone application and conducted via video or phone. Depending on with which company a person was insured, they could have, during the period when I worked there, between five and eight 30-minute counselling sessions a year. When using the counselling part of the service, the person could choose to use their annual entitlement of sessions in any way they chose, although they were discouraged from seeing more than one practitioner at a time and having more than one session a week. From what I could tell, modal number of counselling sessions people had was '1'. I was a counsellor for 'Scimitar Health' from March 2022 until April 2023 and typically offered between 25 and 50 half-hour sessions monthly.

The Process

When clients booked a counselling session, they did so on the app on their phone. They could see the appointment times available for consultations and the counsellors that were available to be seen at those times. Each counsellor had a short biographical statement next to their name. Mine was:

> *'I am Emeritus Professor of Psychotherapeutic Studies at Goldsmiths University of London. I am a Fellow of the British Psychological Society (BPS) and the British Association for Counselling and Psychotherapy (BACP). I am the developer of ONEplus therapy. This means that I will work with you to help you take away something that will make a difference in your life due to our conversation (the 'ONE'). If you need more help, that is fine too, and you can always talk to me again or to one of my colleagues (the 'plus'). I aim to help you make the most out of every session we have together – one or more.'*

This indicated my interest in single-session therapy (which I referred to as 'ONEplus therapy – see Dryden, 2023a, 2023b and Chapter 8) and made clear that I would work to help the person take away what they had come for from the session but that more help (up to six or eight sessions depending on the company with which they are insured) was available to them (Dryden, 2024a).

'Scimitar Health' did not explicitly offer single-session therapy by design. However, its utilization patterns suggest that its work could be best characterized as single-session therapy by default.

Problem Categories

When a booking was made, the counsellor could view the client's portal page, and here, the client's issue was listed as being one of the following: 'anxiety', 'depression/low mood', 'stress', 'bereavement' and 'other'. Only individual counselling of adults was permitted in the service.

Preparing for an Online Counselling Session

When I received a booking sent to my company email account I emailed the person as follows:

> Dear
>
> We have a 30-minute video counselling session booked through 'Scimitar Health' on (date and time), and I look forward to meeting you.
>
> You access the session through the app.
>
> I have found it helpful to ask clients to prepare for their session with me, and to that effect, I would be grateful if you would download and complete **the attached form**. Let me emphasise that this is not mandatory; it is just something that will help you get the most from our session. If you decide to complete it, I would be grateful if you would share a copy with me by email attachment so I can prepare for our session too. Please send it back as a Word document

or as a PDF.

Please be in an indoor, private space with no disruptions and a good internet connection. It does not work to have a counselling session in a coffee bar, in a car (even when stationary) or in an outside space. It is also not appropriate for you to be in your bedroom when having a counselling session.

Best wishes,

Windy Dryden

As the email clarified, I outlined the netiquette[49] of having an online session with me. I also invited the person who had booked a session with me to complete an attached form which is the pre-session questionnaire (PSQ) – see Table 1.4 in Chapter 1. I stressed that the purpose of completing the PSQ was to help the person prepare for the session so that they could get the most from it. I also invited them to send me the completed form so that I could prepare for the session. I stressed that its completion was not mandatory. Approximately 80% of people completed and returned the questionnaire. There was a high correlation between those who don't return the PSQ and those who cancelled or failed to attend the session.

As far as I am aware, I was the only 'Scimitar Health' counsellor to ask clients to prepare for what was probably the only session that they would have (see the section below on 'The Modal Number of My Sessions is '1'').

Type of Help Requested by Clients

Norcross and Cooper (2022) argue and provide data to support the contention that effective therapy is more likely to occur when the client receives the type of help they seek from the therapist than when they receive a different type of help. To provide clients with the help they wanted from the session, I asked them to

---

[49] *Netiquette* describes the rules of conduct for respectful and appropriate online communication.

specify this on the PSQ. Table 12.1 outlines the help requested by a sample of 300 people who booked a counselling session with me between March 2022 and April 2023. This shows clearly that the most frequent form of help requested by this cohort was for a specific emotional or behavioural problem with which the person had become stuck. However, as Table 12.1 also shows, a minority of clients sought a different form of help. As someone guided by single-session thinking (e.g., Cannistrà, 2022), I aimed to offer each client the help they wanted rather than the help I thought they needed.

Table 12.1   Type of help wanted (N = 300) (Pre-session Questionnaire – select one)

Category	Number	%
Help me to solve an emotional or behavioural problem; help me get unstuck	163	54.3%
More than one category specified	58	19.3%
Help me to develop a greater understanding of the issue	37	12.3%
Other	13	4.3%
No category specified	9	3.0%
Help me to express my feelings about the issue	7	2.3%
Help me to make a decision	7	2.3%
Help me to resolve a dilemma	4	1.3%
Just listen while I talk about the issue	2	0.7%

Thirty-Minute Sessions

'Scimitar Health' only offered clients thirty-minute counselling sessions. While this may be considered relatively short compared to the 'standard' fifty-minute therapy session, I found it quite ample given my experience conducting demonstrations of single-session therapy in training workshops (Dryden, 2018). In over 750 such sessions, the average session length was 22 minutes 14 seconds. Thus, I am used to helping clients get what they want from a counselling session within the thirty minutes allotted to counsellors.

The Modal Number of My Sessions is '1'

As I have already stated, while seventy counsellors worked for 'Scimitar Health', I knew very little about the nature of the work they did and what the modal number of their sessions was. The data that I am now going to present concerns only the work that I did for the organisation.

From March 2022 to April 2023, I saw 463 'Scimitar Health' clients for 601 sessions. Figure 12.1 outlines the number of people I saw in that period and the number of sessions I had with them. As can be seen, the modal number of sessions that I had with clients was '1'. However, I do not know if clients sought further help from other counsellors in the service because such data were not available to individual practitioners.

Figure 12.1 Modal number of sessions (N = 601) carried out by Windy Dryden for 'Scimitar Health' from March 2022–April 2023

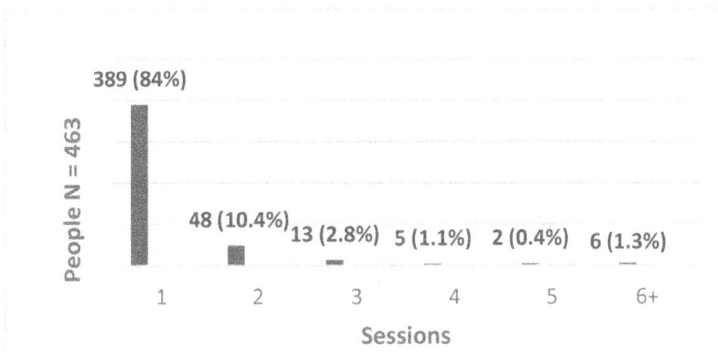

The Case of 'George'

As an example of the counselling work I did for 'Scimitar Health', I will present the case of 'George' (a pseudonym). George was a 31-year-old man who listed his problem as 'Other'. As described above, I sent George an email requesting that he prepare for the session by completing the Pre-Session Questionnaire (PSQ) and returning it to me so I could prepare for the session.

George's PSQ

George reported having an issue with binge drinking, which led him to neglect his friends and girlfriend. Occasionally, he drank so much that he blacked out and could not remember what happened to him. He had not up to the time I saw him gotten into trouble but he recognised that he was putting himself at risk by drinking the way he did. He wanted to discuss the issue with a neutral party to see if there was a reason for his behaviour and to discover 'good methods for dealing with this'. He wanted to learn how to go out drinking with his friends without getting 'blackout' drunk. He mentioned that he did not seem to have great self-control and struggled to say 'No' to people. He also said that he used to be shy and was now more confident but used alcohol to help him with his confidence.

In response to the question concerning what he had done to deal with the issue, George replied that he had tried tracking his use of alcohol on nights out and setting himself limits. When he did reduce his alcohol intake use, he later rewarded himself by drinking more on subsequent nights out.

Outlining the strengths that he had that he could use to address the issue, George said that he had a scientific outlook and liked to know the why of things. He also said that he was competitive and did not like to lose. Listing the people in his life who could help him with the issue, George mentioned his girlfriend, three male friends and his father, who all listened to him and tried to reassure him. Finally, George listed 'help me to solve an emotional or behavioural problem; help me get unstuck' as the type of help he wanted from me.

The Session

In the session, I asked George to nominate a specific example that we could work with to understand what was going on. His most significant vulnerability was to participate in drinking games, and when he did so, he realised that his 'competitive self' believed that he had to win them. Here, he saw that what he considered one of his strengths was maintaining the problem. George also realised that while participating in these games, he was ordering drinks for himself so that he was drinking twice as much as he wanted. We dealt with his fear of missing out ('FOMO'), and he realised he could enjoy himself without engaging in drinking games. Not wanting to disappoint others was another factor here, but I helped him see that his friends would still like him if he chose not to participate in drinking games or decided to drink less and that if any of his friends stopped liking him, they were not his true friends. He also concluded that he would not order drinks outside of the game if he chose to engage in a drinking game.

I distinguished between distal and proximal factors, which George thought was helpful. His distal factors were why he wanted to control his drinking – not wanting to worry his girlfriend and not wanting to be vulnerable when he was 'blackout' drunk. However, while these factors were important, they did not help him deal with the proximal factors – the factors that he faced in the moment (e.g., dealing with disappointing his friends, not wanting to miss out and ordering drinks outside of drinking games while having drinking drinks in these games).

I helped him deal with these proximal factors in imagery so that he could practise assertion and self-control. For example, he imagined being invited to join a drinking game when he was out and rehearsed the idea that he didn't need to accept this invitation, even if his friends seemed disappointed. Then he pictured himself saying 'No' to the game. He then pictured himself feeling uncomfortable about missing out on the fun but reminded himself that he was doing so to protect his well-being and repay the trust placed in him by his girlfriend. He resolved to rehearse this imagery method daily and at the beginning of an evening out.

Finally, I helped George see that while he had tried in the past to deal logically with his issue (e.g., monitoring his alcohol intake and setting limits on his drinking), these had not been successful because he had not dealt with the psychological factors that we discussed in the session. This explanation, he said, appealed to his 'scientific nature'. At the end of the session, George said that he had got what he had come for and would seek further help if he needed to in the future.[50]

'Claire's' Perspective

'Claire' (a pseudonym) was another client I saw through my work with 'Scimitar Health'. What follows is her account of the session she had with me put into the context of her life.

'I myself am a counsellor, but I came to this single session model when I needed help personally. I reached out for help after a difficult interaction with my Mum left me shaken and was getting in the way of me reaching out to people professionally.

I had been excited and confident about new business plans when I shared them with my Mum. We have a difficult relationship and she is often critical. On this occasion, I'd let myself believe she might be encouraging, so her evident disapproval and lack of support stung. It left me feeling rejected and like a child again seeking validation. I needed to believe in myself to move forward, but her criticism had derailed me.

This became a problem on the work front when I noticed myself avoiding the influential people I wanted to reach out to. I was holding back and wanted to keep all my ideas safe inside me. I knew my relationship with my critical and opinionated Mum was at the heart of all this. But this insight wasn't helping me do things differently. I didn't want or have the capacity for long-term therapy. I wanted a shortcut back to "me" after this recent incident at a critical time had shaken my sense of self and identity. I was just tired, a bit lost and needing a strategy.

I received the questionnaire[51] several days before my planned session with Windy. Filling it out saved me. Taking

---

[50] As I will discuss below, 'Scimitar Health' did not attempt to gain outcome data from its clients so at present, I do not know what use George made of the session.

[51] This refers to the Pre-Session Questionnaire discussed earlier.

time to reflect on my problem prevented me from falling into an age-old trap. The trap of spending time and energy trying to make it "right" with my Mum, of desperately trying to change her mind and alter her perception of me. I still did this from time to time, even after years of boundary-setting and long-term therapy and knowing full well we can't change what others choose to see.

Under the question, "How have you tried to deal with the issue up to this point?" I wrote everything I knew helped (which was helpful), then lastly,

I've also tried engaging with and speaking with her about this – this has never been successful!

Seeing this written down in black and white had a big impact. "Oh" I thought to myself, I HAVE tried this endlessly and doggedly for years. Every time it fails to help and actually harms me. Clear that I shouldn't go there, this galvanised me to look for solutions elsewhere.

While I didn't relish the "work" involved in writing about my problems, it was helpful to list my resources and strengths and get things out of my head and onto paper. It brought lightness and clarity to something that had felt heavy and messy. I'm not one for journaling, even though I know it's helpful. Here I got the benefits of journaling but with helpful structured questions to help me pinpoint the problem and accountability. I felt ready for our session and hopeful about the change it promised.

I had already identified the crux of my problem and knew what I wanted via a questionnaire, so we had a productive start. Though I didn't know Windy, I immediately felt comfortable and knew he genuinely wanted to understand me and my problem in order to help. We didn't discuss my Mum, just what I wanted to achieve which was a simple strategy to shore me up and hold in mind as I reached out with my work. Using an upcoming real-life situation as an example, we imagined how I'd feel and what I could do differently. I felt supported yet challenged to stay focused. This didn't feel like a holding space. It felt like a safe space to imagine and do.

It became clear that I had a perspective problem. I saw myself as "less than" the "important" people I wanted to engage. I wanted a way to elevate my view of myself. Windy suggested something I couldn't see: I could change how I see others by humanising them, metaphorically bringing them down to size, too. I envisioned myself as a bit bigger AND others as essentially human like me. We also prepared for dismissal from some busy people because that was the likely reality. I realised dismissal itself wasn't a problem; it was linking rejection to feeling unworthy and small that hindered me. I could feel differently after any rejection, so be free to proceed confidently. Resizing my perception of myself and others would allow me to reach out effectively. As a therapist used to 50-minute sessions, I was struck that we hadn't even used our half hour. I left hopeful, with a clear plan to apply this perspective shift.

Professionally, it completely changed the way I work. I retrained to offer Single-Session Therapy to ensure more people aren't left waiting and get help at the time of need. My experience of being let down by a system that had promised to support led me to rethink what we need from the systems themselves. I do now believe that, sometimes, one session working in a focussed and intentional way is all the support they need.

I now know that things go well for me when I feel an appropriate size in professional relationships. I know to mentally "right-size" people whenever things feel out of whack. This has helped hugely as I establish myself in my work and bring my ideas to the world. As I write, it's clear I should try this technique with my Mum now, too. Half an hour of therapeutic time well spent had a huge impact. And time spent in preparation and reflection has as well.'

Organisational Factors

Jeff Young (2018) has pointed out that single-session therapy occurs in a given context. When that context is an organisation, the 'health' of that organisation will impact whether the practice of single-session therapy will flourish or wither. So, let me end this chapter by discussing the aspects of 'Scimitar Health' that facilitate the work I did for the organisation and those that detracted from that work.

Features of 'Scimitar Health' that Facilitated My Work
One of the biggest drivers in my work life is autonomy. Most of the time, I know what I am doing and want to be left alone to do it. Given that all counsellors who worked for 'Scimitar Health' were self-employed, we were autonomous about how we

practised, but, of course, we had to work within organisational guidelines, which, in the period covered by this chapter was that we offered between 5 and 8 sessions to each client annually depending upon by which insurance company they were covered. This meant I could work as much or as little as I wanted and practised as I wanted (within the above-mentioned constraints). On this latter point, I brought a single-session mindset to the work and clarified this in my biographical statement. My main aim was to help each client take away from the session the help they specified on my Pre-Session Questionnaire (PSQ), which I had permission from the organisation to send out to a person once I had received their booking (see Postscript).

The best aspect of my work for 'Scimitar Health' was that I loved it and would have been loathe to give it up (although see below for a discussion of factors that detracted from my work). I considered that there was a lot that I could do with a client who came to the 30-minute session duly prepared to work with me to get the most from the session. In short, being a counsellor for 'Scimitar Health' allowed me to help a range of people while bringing a single-session mindset to this work.

Features of 'Scimitar Health' that Detracted from My Work

However, my experience taught me that there was also a downside to working for 'Scimitar Health'. First, given that counsellors were self-employed, the organisation did not supervise our counselling work, arguing that this is our responsibility given our self-employed status. They made no checks on whether counsellors sought clinical supervision and did not know if our supervisors were skilled at the work that we did so that they could offer us informed supervision.

Second, in the period covered by this chapter (March 2022– April 2023), 'Scimitar Health' did not provide counsellors with any clinical leadership for our work. Clinical leads (as they are known) are typically responsible for overseeing the delivery of high-quality client care and implementing best practices and guidelines to ensure that clinical standards are maintained. The role of a supervisor is to give a counsellor *specific* feedback on their work with clients, while the role of a clinical lead is to provide *general* guidance on clinical standards. The company's clinical lead in this period was a medical general practitioner who was not professionally trained as a counsellor. Consequently, counsellors were left without the clinical guidance they could reasonably have expected from an organisation such as 'Scimitar Health'. Subsequently, the organisation appointed two counsellors to join a clinical oversight team whose duties (at the time of writing) had not been clarified for the counsellors.

Third, in the designated period, counsellors had no opportunity to talk to one another about therapeutic matters raised by working for the organisation. This lack of an appropriate forum meant that counsellors were isolated and lacked the support that is, in my view, necessary for those working for an organisation such as 'Scimitar Health'.

Fourth, the 30-minute video sessions - or phone calls if there were connection issues – were recorded and were kept by the company for an unspecified period for safeguarding purposes or if there is a complaint. Clients gave their informed consent for these recordings to be made. However, if they refrained from doing so, the session did not take place. These recordings could have been used – with permission – for training and development purposes but this was not done.

Fifth, the organisation did not attempt to collect data from clients to assess the outcome of counselling, and there was no evaluation of individual counsellors' performance. Thus, if the organisation were to be asked about the effectiveness of its counselling service or how it discriminates between effective and ineffective counsellors, it could not answer such questions. That said, as a practitioner, I asked clients at the end of the session if they had gotten what they had come for and how they planned to implement their takeaways.

I did try to address the above five issues with the organisation but did not have satisfactory responses, and in some cases, my questions were unanswered. I was constantly wavering between continuing to do the work I loved and working for an organisation I was critical of. Despite these frustrations, it was a delight to be able to help clients often in one session.

Postscript

While I was attending the 4th International Symposium on Single-Session Therapy in Rome in November 2023, I and other counsellors working for 'Scimitar Health' received an email stating that given the changes that had been recently made to service provision, counsellors were only allowed to have contact with clients during counselling sessions or through the Silver Cloud portal.[52] This seemed to mean that I would no longer be able to send my welcome email to clients who had booked in to see me and the pre-session questionnaire presented in Table 12.1, even though I had previous permission to do so and had done so for over a year. The newly appointed Clinical Lead confirmed this. This proved to be the tipping point for me, and I tendered my resignation in November 2023.

'Scimitar Health's position on counsellor-client contact meant to me the following:

1. I could not welcome clients who had booked a session with me.
2. I could not outline the 'netiquette' of online counselling to clients.
3. Most importantly, I could not ask clients to prepare to get the most from the session by completing my pre-session questionnaire.
4. I could not send clients any relevant information after the session.

While I loved the work, I had reached a point where the 'fit' between myself as a practitioner, and 'Scimitar Health' as the host organisation was not a sustainable one.

We can expect online SST to expand in the future, and I hope the experiences outlined here will help to make online SST optimally useful.

---

[52] Silver Cloud is a digital mental health and wellbeing platform providing digital Cognitive Behavioural Therapy (CBT) programmes and tools.

Appendix 1

Publications on Single-Session Therapy and Very Brief Therapeutic Work

Windy Dryden

Books

Dryden, W. (1996). *Rational Emotive Behaviour Therapy: Learning from Demonstration Sessions*. Whurr Publishers.

Dryden, W., & Ellis, A. (2003). *Albert Ellis Live!* Sage.

Dryden, W. (2016). *When Time is at a Premium: Cognitive-Behavioural Approaches to Single-Session Therapy and Very Brief Coaching*. Rationality Publications.

Dryden, W. (2017). *Single-Session Integrated CBT (SSI-CBT): Distinctive Features*. Routledge.

Dryden, W. (2017). *Very Brief Cognitive-Behavioural Coaching (VBCBC)*. Routledge.

Dryden, W. (2018). *Very Brief Therapeutic Conversations*. Routledge.

Dryden, W. (2019). *Single-Session Therapy: 100 Key Points and Techniques*. Routledge.

Dryden, W. (2019). *Single-Session Therapy: Distinctive Features*. Routledge.

Dryden, W. (2019). *Single-Session 'One-At-A-Time' (OAAT) Therapy: A Rational Emotive Behaviour Therapy Approach*. Routledge.

Dryden, W. (2019). *REBT in India: Very Brief Therapy for Problems of Daily Living*. Routledge.

Dryden, W. (2020). *Single-Session Coaching and One-At-A-Time Coaching: Distinctive features*. Routledge.

Dryden, W. (2020). *The Single-Session Counselling Primer: Principles and Practice*. PCCS Books.

Dryden, W. (2021). *Single-Session Therapy and its Future: What SST Leaders Think*. Routledge.

Dryden, W. (2021). *Help Yourself with Single-Session Therapy*. Routledge.

Dryden, W. (2021). *Seven Principles of Single-Session Therapy*. Rationality Publications.

Dryden, W. (2021). *Windy Dryden Live!* Rationality Publications.

Dryden, W. (2021). *Seven Principles of Doing Live Therapy Demonstrations.* Rationality Publications.

Dryden, W. (2021). *Single-Session Therapy @ Onlinevents.* Onlinevents Publications.

Dryden, W. (2021). *The Single-Session Therapist's Pocket Companion.* Rationality Publications.

Dryden, W. (2022). *Single-Session Therapy: Responses to Frequently Asked Questions.* Routledge.

Dryden, W. (2022). *Single-Session Integrated CBT (SSI-CBT): Distinctive Features. 2nd Edition.* Routledge.

Dryden, W. (2022). *'I Wish You a Healthy Christmas': Single-Session Therapy in Action.* Onlinevents Publications.

Dryden, W. (2023). *Single-Session Therapy and Regret.* Onlinevents Publications.

Dryden, W. (2023). *ONEplus Therapy: Help at the Point of Need.* Onlinevents Publications.

Dryden, W. (2024). *Single-Session Therapy: 100 Key Points and Techniques. 2nd Edition* Routledge.

Dryden, W. (2024). *Single-Session Therapy: Distinctive Features. 2nd Edition.* Routledge.

Dryden, W. (2024). *Single-Session Therapy and Procrastination.* Onlinevents Publications.

Dryden, W. (2024). *ONEplus Therapy and Common Emotional Problems.* Onlinevents Publications.

Dryden, W. (2024). *How to Think and Intervene Like a Single-Session Therapist.* Routledge.

Booklet

Dryden, W. (2019). *Single-Session Therapy (SST) and One-At-A-Time (OAAT): Help at the Point of Need.* Rationality Publications.

Articles

Dryden, W. (2010). Two REBT therapists and one client: Windy Dryden transcript. *Journal of Rational-Emotive and Cognitive-Behavior Therapy, 28*(3), 130–40.

Dryden, W. (2010). Elegance in REBT: Reflections on the Ellis and Dryden sessions with Jane. *Journal of Rational-Emotive and Cognitive-Behavior Therapy, 28*(3), 157–63.

Dryden, W. (2012). Dealing with procrastination: The REBT approach and a demonstration session. *Journal of Rational-Emotive & Cognitive-Behavior Therapy, 30,* 264–81.

Dryden, W. (2019). It forced me to think in different ways about single session therapy. *The Psychologist, 32*(11), 44–6; also *The Psychologist Online.* https://thepsychologist.bps.org.uk/it-forced-me-think-different-ways about-single-session-therapy

Dryden W. (2020). Providing help at the point of need: Insights from single-session therapy. *University and College Counselling, May,* 28–31.

Dryden, W. (2020). Not all clients need or want a deep relationship with their counsellors: The Big Interview with Catherine Jackson. *Therapy Today,* July, 24–27.

Dryden, W. (2020). Single-session one at-a-time therapy: A personal approach. *Australian and New Zealand Journal of Family Therapy, 41,* 283–301. DOI: 10.1002/anzf.1424.

Dryden, W. (2020). Skills in single-session therapy. Part 1: Creating and maintaining a focus. *European Journal of Counselling Theory, Research and Practice, 4*(4), 1–4. http://www.europeancounselling.eu/volumes/volume-4-2020/volume-4-article-4/

Dryden, W. (2021). Single-session counselling. Accord, 110, 36-39.

Dryden, W. (2022). Skills in single-session therapy. Part 2: Ways of Beginning the Session. *European Journal of Counselling Theory, Research and Practice, 6*(3), 1–4. https://ejctrap.nationalwellbeingservice.com/volumes/volume-6-2022/volume-6-article-3/

Dryden, W. (2023). What's in a name? What to call therapy when a client may come once. *Inside Out, 100,* 12–14.

Dryden, W. (2023). Single-session therapy and the therapist's fear of opening up a can of worms. *Inside Out, 101,* 37–9.

Dryden, W. (2024). Skills in Single-Session Therapy. Part 3: Ways of working with problems and solutions. *European Journal of Counselling Theory, Research and Practice, 8*(2), 1–6. https://ejctrap.nationalwellbeingservice.com/volumes/volume-8-2024/volume-8-article-2

Dryden, W. (2024). Skills in Single-Session Therapy. Part 4: Ways of ending the session. *European Journal of Counselling Theory, Research and Practice, 8*(3), 1–4. https://ejctrap.nationalwellbeingservice.com/volumes/volume-8-2024/volume-8-article-3

Hoyt, M.F., & Dryden, W. (2018). Toward the future of single-session therapy: An Interview. *Journal of Systemic Therapies, 37*(1), 79–89.

Young, J., & Dryden, W (2019). Single-session therapy – past and future: An interview. *British Journal of Guidance and Counselling, 47*(5), 645–54. DOI: 10.1080/03069885.2019.1581129

Chapters

Dryden, W. (2021). Sign up, meet up, speak out: Single sessions in the context of meet-up groups. In M.F. Hoyt, J. Young & P. Rycroft (eds), *Single Session Thinking and Practice in Global, Cultural and Familial Contexts: Expanding Applications* (pp. 153–62). Routledge.

Dryden, (2022). Capturing and making use of the Moment: REBT-informed single-session therapy. In W. Dryden (ed.), *New Directions in Rational Emotive Behaviour Therapy* (pp. 55–76). Routledge.

Dryden, W. (2022). Single-session, cognitive-behavioural coaching (SSCBC). In M. Neenan & S. Palmer (eds), *Cognitive Behavioural Coaching in Practice: An Evidence-Based Approach. 2nd Edition.* (pp. 221–42). Routledge.

Dryden, W. (2022). New ideas: One-at-a-time therapy. In S. Bennett, P. Myles-Hooton & J. Schleider (eds), *Oxford Guide to Low-Intensity Evidence-Based Interventions for Children and Young People.* Oxford University Press.

Dryden, W. (2025). Bringing a single-session mindset to counselling in an online health service in the UK. In Hoyt, M.F. & Cannistra, F. (eds). *Single Session Therapies: Why and How One-At-A-Time Mindsets are Effective.* Routledge.

Appendix 2

The Conventional Therapy Mindset

- Therapy is likely to take time to yield a benefit for clients.

- It is vital to provide ongoing therapy for some clients and an agreed number of sessions for others. The purpose of the first session is to help the therapist to determine which mode of therapy is suitable for which client.

- The more complex and severe the client's problems, the longer they will need to be in therapy.

- Many clients benefit from having a relationship of depth with their therapists, Such a relationship takes a while to develop, and in some cases, it will take months or years.

- Clients generally need time to get used to being in therapy.

- Clients need to talk about whatever they wish, particularly at the beginning, and therapists should allow them to do this.

- The early phase of therapy should be taken up with assessing the client, taking a case history and developing a case formulation.

- The purpose of the first psychotherapy session is to encourage the client to come back for a second.

- A client's problems will be resolved when they have worked through these through the transference. This requires time.

- Clients need to learn new skills from therapy; this takes time.

- Empirically supported treatments require multiple sessions.

- A client's initial *presenting* problems are not as significant as their real problems, which they will take time to reveal.

References

Appelbaum, S.A. (1975). Parkinson's Law in psychotherapy. *International Journal of Psychoanalytic Psychotherapy,* 4, 426–36.

Bloom, B.L. (1981). Focused single-session therapy: Initial development and evaluation. In S. Budman (ed.), *Forms of Brief Therapy* (pp. 167–216). Guilford Press.

Bloom, B.L. (1992). *Planned Short-Term Psychotherapy: A Clinical Handbook.* Allyn and Bacon.

Bloom, B.L. (2001). Focused single session psychotherapy: A review of the clinical and research literature. *Brief Treatment and Crisis Intervention,* 1(1), 75–86.

Bordin, E.S. (1979). The generalizability of the psychoanalytic concept of the working alliance. *Psychotherapy: Theory, Research and Practice, 16*(3): 252–60.

Brown, G.S., & Jones, E.R. (2005). Implementation of a feedback system in a managed care environment: What are patients teaching us? *Journal of Clinical Psychology, 61,* 187–98.

Campbell, A. (2012). Single-session approaches to therapy: Time to review. *Australian and New Zealand Journal of Family Therapy,* 33(1), 15–26.

Cannistrà, F. (2022). The single session therapy mindset: Fourteen principles gained through an analysis of the literature. *International Journal of Brief Therapy and Family Science, 12* (1), 1–26.

Cummings, N.A. (1990). Brief intermittent psychotherapy through the life cycle. In, J.K. Zeig & S.G Gilligan (eds), *Brief Therapy: Myths, Methods and Metaphors* (pp. 169–94). Brunner/Mazel.

Curran, J., Parry, G.D., Hardy, G.E., Darling, J., Mason, A-M., & Chambers, E. (2019). How does therapy harm? A model of adverse process using task analysis in the meta-synthesis of service users' experience. *Frontiers in Psychology, 10,* 347. ISSN 1664-1078. https://doi.org/10.3389/fpsyg.2019.00347.

DiGiuseppe, R. (1991). The rational-emotive model of assessment. In: M. Bernard (Ed.), *Using Rational–Emotive Therapy Effectively* (pp. 151–72). Plenum.

Dryden, W. (1986). Vivid methods in rational-emotive therapy. In A. Ellis & R. Grieger (eds), *Handbook of Rational-Emotive Therapy. Volume 2* (pp. 221–45). Springer.

Dryden, W. (2000). *Overcoming Procrastination.* Sheldon Press.

Dryden, W. (2008). *Overcoming Procrastination: Master Therapists DVD Series.* Albert Ellis Institute.

Dryden, W (2010). Two REBT therapists and one client: Windy Dryden transcript. *Journal of Rational-Emotive and Cognitive-Behavior Therapy, 28*(3), 130–40.

Dryden, W. (2011). *Counselling in a Nutshell. 2nd Edition.* Sage.

Dryden, W. (2012). Dealing with procrastination: The REBT approach and a demonstration session. *Journal of Rational-Emotive & Cognitive-Behavior Therapy, 30,* 264–81.

Dryden, W. (2017). *Single-Session Integrated CBT (SSI-CBT): Distinctive Features.* Routledge.

Dryden, W. (2018). *Very Brief Therapeutic Conversations.* Routledge.

Dryden, W. (2019). *Single-Session 'One-At-A-Time' (OAAT) Therapy: A Rational Emotive Behaviour Therapy Approach.* Routledge.

Dryden, W. (2020). *The Single-Session Therapy Primer: Principles and Practice.* PCCS Books.

Dryden, W. (2021a). *Seven Principles of Doing Live Therapy Demonstrations.* Rationality Publications.

Dryden, W. (2021b). *Windy Dryden Live!* Rationality Publications.

Dryden, W (2022a). *Overcoming Procrastination. 2nd Edition.* Sheldon Press.

Dryden, W. (2022b). *Single-Session Integrated CBT (SSI-CBT): Distinctive Features. 2nd Edition.* Routledge.

Dryden, W. (2022c). *Single-Session Therapy: Responses to Frequently Asked Questions.* Routledge.

Dryden, W. (2023a). *ONEplus Therapy: Help at the Point of Need.* Onlinevents Publications.

Dryden, W. (2023b). What's in a name? What to call therapy when a client may come once. *Inside Out, 100,* 12–14.

Dryden, W. (2024a). *Single-Session Therapy: 100 Key Points and Techniques* (2nd edition). Routledge.

Dryden, W. (2024b). *Single-Session Therapy and Procrastination.* Onlinevents.

Dryden, W. (2025). Bringing a single-session mindset to counselling in an online health service. In F. Cannistrà & M.F. Hoyt (eds), *Single Session Therapies: Why and How One-At-A-Time Mindsets Are Effective.* Routledge.

Ellis, A. (1989). Ineffective consumerism in the cognitive-behavioural therapies and in general psychotherapy. In W. Dryden & P. Trower (eds), *Cognitive Psychotherapy: Stasis and Change* (pp. 159–74). Cassell.

Ellis, A., & Joffe, D. (2002). A study of volunteer clients who experienced live sessions of rational emotive behavior therapy in front of a public audience. *Journal of Rational-Emotive & Cognitive-Behavior Therapy, 20,* 151–8.

Frank, J.D. (1961). *Persuasion and Healing: A Comprehensive Study of Psychotherapy*. The Johns Hopkins Press.

Freud, S. & Breuer, J. (1895). *Studien Über Hysterie*. Deuticke.

Hardy, G. E., Bishop-Edwards, L., Chambers, E., Connell, J., Dent-Brown, K., Kothari, G., O'Hara, R. & Parry, G.D. (2017). Risk factors for negative experiences during psychotherapy. *Psychotherapy Research, 27*, 1–12.

Hoyt, M.F. (2000). *Some Stories are Better than Others: Doing What Works in Brief Therapy and Managed Care*. Brunner/ Mazel.

Hoyt, M. F. (2011). Foreword. In A. Slive & M. Bobele (eds), *When One Hour Is All You Have: Effective Therapy for Walk-in Clients* (pp. xix–xv). Zeig, Tucker, & Theisen.

Hoyt, M.F. (2018). Single-session therapy: Stories, structures, themes, cautions, and prospects. In M.F. Hoyt, M. Bobele, A. Slive, J. Young, J., & M. Talmon (eds), *Single-Session Therapy by Walk-In or Appointment: Administrative, Clinical, and Supervisory Aspects of One-at- a-Time Services* (pp. 155–74). Routledge.

Hoyt, M.F., Bobele, M., Slive, A., Young, J., & Talmon, M. (2018). Introduction: One at-a-time/single-session walk-in therapy. In M.F. Hoyt, M. Bobele, A. Slive, J. Young, J., & M. Talmon (eds), *Single-Session Therapy by Walk-In or Appointment: Administrative, Clinical, and Supervisory Aspects of One-at-a-Time Services* (pp. 3–24). Routledge.

Hoyt, M.F, & Rosenbaum, R. (2018). Some ways to end an SST. In M.F. Hoyt, M. Bobele, A. Slive, J. Young, & M. Talmon (Eds.), *Single-Session Therapy by Walk-In or Appointment: Administrative, Clinical, and Supervisory Aspects of One-at-a-Time Services* (pp. 318–23). Routledge.

Hoyt, M.F., Rosenbaum, R., & Talmon, M. (1992). Planned single-session psychotherapy. In S.H. Budman, M.F. Hoyt, & S. Friedman (eds), *The First Session in Brief Therapy* (pp. 59–86). Guilford Press.

Hoyt, M.F., & Talmon, M.F. (eds) (2014a). *Capturing the Moment: Single Session Therapy and Walk-in Services*. Crown House Publishing.

Hoyt, M.F., & Talmon, M.F. (2014b). What the literature says: An annotated bibliography. In M.F. Hoyt & M. Talmon (eds), *Capturing the Moment: Single Session Therapy and Walk-in Services* (pp. 487–516). Crown House Publishing.

Hoyt, M.F., Young, J., & Rycroft, P. (eds) (2021). *Single Session Thinking and Practice in Global, Cultural and Familial Contexts: Expanding Applications*. Routledge.

Hymmen, P., Stalker, C.A., & Cait, C-A. (2013). The case for single-session therapy: Does the empirical evidence support the increased prevalence of this service delivery model? *Journal of Mental Health,* 22(1): 60–7.

Lilienfeld, S.O. (2007). Psychological treatments that cause harm. *Perspectives on Psychological Science, 2,* 53–70.

Miller, W.R. & C' de Baca, J. (2001). *Quantum Change: When Epiphanies and Sudden Insights Transform Ordinary Lives.* Guilford.

Murphy, J.J., & Sparks, J.A. (2018). *Strengths-Based Therapy: Distinctive Features.* Routledge.

Norcross, J.C., & Cooper, M. (2021). *Personalizing Psychotherapy: Assessing and Accommodating Patient Preferences.* American Psychological Association.

Parry, G.D., Crawford, M.J. & Duggan, C. (2016). Iatrogenic harm from psychological therapies–time to move on. *British Journal of Psychiatry, 208,* 210–12.

Pugh, M. (2021). Single-session chairwork: Overview and case illustration of brief dialogical psychotherapy. *British Journal of Guidance & Therapy,*
DOI: 10.1080/03069885.2021.1984395.

Schleider, J.L., Dobias, M.L., Sung, J.Y., & Mullarkey, M.C. (2020). Future directions in single-session youth mental health interventions. *Journal of Clinical Child and Adolescent Psychology, 49,* 264–78.

Shostrom, E.L. (Producer). (1965). *Three Approaches to Psychotherapy, Series I [Motion picture].* (Available from Psychological & Educational Films, 3334 East Coast Highway #252, Corona Del Mar, CA 92625).

Simon, G.E., Imel, Z.E., Ludman, E.J., & Steinfeld, B.J. (2012). Is dropout after a first psychotherapy visit always a bad outcome? *Psychiatric Services, 63*(7), 705–7.

Slive, A., & Bobele, M. (eds) (2011). *When One Hour Is All You Have: Effective Therapy for Walk-in Clients.* Zeig, Tucker & Theisen.

Slive, A., & Bobele, M. (2014). Walk-in single-session therapy: Accessible mental health services. In M.F. Hoyt & M. Talmon (eds), *Capturing the Moment: Single Session Therapy and Walk-in Services* (pp. 73–94). Crown House Publishing.

Talmon, M. (1990). *Single Session Therapy: Maximising the Effect of the First (and Often Only) Therapeutic Encounter.* Jossey-Bass.

Talmon, M. (1993). *Single Session Solutions: A Guide to Practical, Effective and Affordable Therapy.* Addison-Wesley.

Talmon, M. (2018). The eternal now: On becoming and being a single-session therapist. In M.F. Hoyt, M. Bobele, A. Slive, J. Young, J., & M. Talmon, (Eds.), *Single-Session Therapy by Walk-In or Appointment: Administrative, Clinical, and Supervisory Aspects of One-at-a-Time Services* (pp. 149-154). Routledge.

Weir, S., Wills, M., Young, J., & Perlesz, A. (2008). *The Implementation of Single Session Work in Community Health.* The Bouverie Centre, La Trobe University.

Young, J. (2018). SST: The misunderstood gift that keeps on giving. In M.F. Hoyt, M. Bobele, A. Slive, J. Young, J., & M. Talmon, (eds), *Single-Session Therapy by Walk-In or Appointment: Administrative, Clinical, and Supervisory Aspects of One-at-a-Time Services* (pp. 40–58). Routledge.

Index

264 *Index*

www.ingramcontent.com/pod-product-compliance
Lightning Source LLC
Chambersburg PA
CBHW060839280326
41934CB00007B/850